Run With Me

Run
With
Me

Sarah Randolph

ISBN: 979-8--9911217-0-5 Paperback
ISBN: 979-8-9911217-1-2 eBook
ISBN:979-8-9911217-2-9 AudioBook

Library of Congress Control Number: TXu2-440-277

Book design by Glen Edelstein, Hudson Valley Book Design

Printed in the United States of America.

First printing edition 2024.

"Saving one dog will not change the world, but surely for that one dog, the world will change forever."
—Karen Davison

For Piper and Brewski...

Introduction

This is the story of two very special dogs who stole the heart of a volunteer dog walker at a local animal shelter. This book explores each dog's background that leads up to them becoming orphans living in a shelter. Their journeys are very different, but when their paths cross at the shelter, they find themselves becoming the best of friends. They take on new adventures together and eventually are faced with leaving the shelter and moving on to the next chapter in their story. This book will delve into the reality of shelter life for dogs, while also providing insight from a volunteer's unique perspective. You will laugh, cry, and wonder why you ever paid top dollar for a pure-bred dog.

My name is Sarah, and I am that volunteer dog walker. I based this book on the real-life experiences I shared with these dogs; however, I created the character of "Brynn" to allow myself to fictionalize certain aspects of my story. Writing the narrative from a different point of view also helped with preventing my emotions from interfering with the direction I wanted to take with this book. I felt compelled to share my story to bring awareness to the overwhelming number of dogs who are living their lives in shelters, waiting to be chosen.

Run With Me was written with the intention of honoring these two very special dogs and using their stories to help as many shelter dogs as possible. By purchasing this book, you are contributing to the welfare of many shelter dogs in need. From one dog lover to another, thank you for your time and generosity. The dogs appreciate it so much!

Prologue

About a quarter of a mile off the road stood an old abandoned house on the outskirts of the city. It was surrounded by a six-foot-tall wooden fence that had seen better days. The house was very run down and the yard was terribly overgrown. A dirt road that led to a winding gravel trail could be accessed from the main road, and the trail ended in front of the gated wooden fence. There were signs posted on the fence warning trespassers to keep out. The house was quite secluded as it sat off the dirt road behind some large pine trees, so it could easily be overlooked if driving by.

Nobody lived in the house but there were two men who dropped in on a daily basis to keep their "business" in order. On occasion there would be a very lavish vehicle that pulled up for a quick transaction inside the house, but the visitors never stayed long. About once a month there was a small group of men who showed up late at night for their entertainment and potential monetary gain. Most days it was just an old, creaky house that was dark and cold inside and void of any furniture or personal belongings. Surprisingly, it was mostly quiet inside, despite the eighteen dogs it housed.

Multiple kennels could be found in every room of the house. Each kennel housed one dog and the dogs were fed and given water daily. All of them were pit bulls or pit bull mixes. One of the female dogs was in the garage with her six new puppies to care for, with a few blankets and a small plastic kid's pool holding the puppies. Injectable steroids, treadmills, and other forms of "conditioning" tools could be found throughout the house. The doors to the house remained locked at all times.

Outside in the front yard were three more dogs. Each dog was chained to the fence with a heavy-duty metal chain connected to a six-inch-wide metal collar around the dog's neck. Each dog had its own house that was shaped like an igloo, with some straw sparsely covering the base of the igloo in case of freezing temperatures. Water dishes were readily available but the water was often frozen in the wintertime. These dogs were the security system for the house. Sometimes they would be rotated with the dogs inside, and sometimes new dogs would come in and old ones would mysteriously disappear. The dogs were never allowed to play with each other, but they did have their ways of communicating, and many of them were the best of friends. They were all each other had.

Late one evening, inside one of the igloos in the front yard slept a black-and-white boy. He was a big boy but was slightly underweight for his stature. He was not a confident dog. He was still young and was very fearful. He was fed daily but didn't always eat because he was too stressed to have much of an appetite. He was asleep in his igloo, but even when sleeping, he was always on high alert. When he heard a door to a vehicle shut nearby, his closed eyes immediately opened wide with fear. His ears perked up and his head tilted to the side, but he didn't move. The other two dogs outside were already barking and he could hear faint barks and cries coming from inside the house.

Darkness surrounded the house and yard. The sky had been overcast that day so there were no stars to provide any light, and there were no outside lights on unless the owners were present, which they were not. The black-and-white boy didn't get up; he remained still until he could determine what was going on. His wide eyes glowed with fright through the darkness of his little house. His brows were furrowed with concern, curiosity, and fear. He wondered who these people were and why they were here. They weren't going to find anyone inside the house. It wasn't an "event" day, as one of the men who operated the business referred to it.

"Anyone here?" a strange voice yelled across the yard. There were two people walking around with flashlights, one man and one woman. As the light got closer to the black-and-white boy's igloo, he cowered as far to the back of his shelter as he could and began to quietly cry. The barking from the other dogs continued to get louder as more dogs became alert to the visitors outside. The woman told the man, "I think we better call for backup before going inside. This is much bigger than we originally thought."

Run With Me

The sound of Brynn's shoes hitting the pavement echoed over and over in her head as she pushed herself harder than usual. It was an early Saturday morning out on the trail and she was training for a half marathon coming up later that summer. The sun was just starting to rise behind her as she ran west into the cool morning air. Her two friends were having a conversation as they all ran side by side, a conversation that felt like it was off in the distance somewhere, drowned by her own thoughts of what had happened the night before. A night she would never forget, nor forgive herself for allowing to happen.

The anger and sadness were so overwhelming. It was propelling her forward faster and harder in her run. Her sunglasses hid her swollen eyes as repetitive visions of what had happened kept replaying in her mind. It was as if her thoughts were in sync with her footsteps hitting the pavement, but she felt the pain with each step taken. She couldn't get the look of terror in Piper's eyes out of her head. She had never seen that look in a dog's eyes before. Those eyes would surely haunt her forever.

Brynn decided she wouldn't say anything to her friends about it. They wouldn't understand. They both had young kids, busy lives. The pain she was feeling wasn't something a lot of her friends or family could really understand or relate to, and she knew that. So she continued to push herself forward. She continued to run with her thoughts.

December 2021

The moment the young dog was walked into the big brick building with a catch pole attached to her neck as if she might attack at any minute, she knew she was finally…safe.

It had been a long two weeks of being on the run, on her own with no shelter, no food or water, no heat. She didn't know what had happened or if she had done something to upset her new owner, but for whatever reason, he had driven her out into the country one day, opened the car door, and pushed her out of it. She had found herself in a strange place she had never seen before, and she was so scared, hungry, cold.

Her eyes followed the taillights of his car as he drove off in the distance. It was dark outside; no streetlights were around to illuminate the area. She walked around lost and confused for what seemed like days, shivering from the cold wind that wouldn't let up. She eventually found an old rickety shed that she was able to use as a makeshift shelter from the cold and snow, but during the daytime she was out wandering, on the hunt for food.

A few days in and the hunger was like nothing she'd ever before experienced. It felt like it had been weeks since she'd last had a meal, but maybe it had only been days. It was hard to tell how much time had passed. The loneliness was starting to get to her too. Why had that man done this to her? Was it punishment for something she had done? She had lived in two different homes in her short life, his being one of them. She had loved her home and family so much, but when her mom got pregnant with their first baby and discovered it was twins, her parents seemed to grow increasingly worried about everything. It was decided that having a young dog in addition to twin babies was going to be too much for them, and that she would have to go to a new home.

She became depressed when she started to figure out what was happening. She tried everything she could to be extra good for them, but the decision had already been made. They had found someone else to take her. He was a friend of a co-worker of her dad's who had been wanting a dog for quite some time. The man came over to their house to meet her one Saturday afternoon, and it seemed like a deal had been made between him and her parents. The couple talked with the man for a long time, shook hands, and exchanged phone numbers.

About a week later, her mom and dad drove her to the man's house with a trunk full of her things. They packed up all her toys, her bed, a blanket she liked to lay on, and some of her favorite treats. They even packed what was left of her thirty-pound bag of specialty food, so she knew she wouldn't be coming back to her home. She was confused as to why this was happening when she was so excited to have twin babies in the family, but she started to realize that it was a done deal.

The mood on the forty-minute drive to the man's house was very solemn. Her mom's eyes had tears that were on the verge of spilling over the entire trip, but she held them back in an effort to stay firm in their decision. They really thought they were doing what was best for their family, and that it would be best to do this while she was still young and more likely to adapt to change. They felt they had found her a good home with this man. On paper this man sounded like a good match for her, but things don't always seem to go as planned.

The man's name was Ed and he was not a very nice man. He was tall with a muscular build, a square jaw, and a stern expression on his face most of the time. It was very rare to see him offer a smile. He was a man of few words, but when he spoke, his voice matched his abrasive personality. It was deep, loud, and intimidating. He demanded obedience from the young female dog and expected nothing less than perfection.

He had a decent home and he fed her twice every day, but once her old bag of specialty food ran out, he didn't feed her the good stuff she had grown accustomed to with her old family. She was convinced he bought the cheapest, nastiest bag of food that was offered at the grocery store. There were no more treats or mid-morning table scraps from her mom eating her eggs and toast at the kitchen table. She no longer got pieces of banana when her dad made a morning smoothie, or baby carrots when he packed his lunch for the day.

Ed left her alone most days while he worked and he didn't ever play fetch with her in the yard or cuddle up on the couch to watch TV with her, or really even talk to her like she existed. It was more like he talked *at* her. He seemed annoyed with her most of the time, like she wasn't the perfect dog he had envisioned in his head. She would sit and stare out the living room window most days while her new owner was at work, wondering if her mom or dad missed her. She missed them so much. They were all she thought of all day while Ed was gone.

She had had a few small accidents in the house on days when Ed had left her alone for over twelve hours at a time. She knew he wasn't happy with her because he had yelled at her and even kicked her in the side with his heavy work boot one night. She had tried her hardest to hold her potty but she was so used to her mom being home to let her outside whenever she gave her the signal that she had to go. Twelve hours is a long time to hold it. She understood that Ed had to work overtime some days, but she just couldn't always hold her potty that long. She had cried out in pain when he kicked her with his boot and couldn't believe he would treat her that badly for something so trivial. But this...she never expected to be dumped in the middle of nowhere, like a bag of trash.

Was it only because she had had those accidents in the house? She wanted to tell him that she would work on holding her potty, that she could do better. At the same time, she wasn't sure she really wanted to do better for such a cruel man. But now what was she going to do? Would anyone ever come looking for her? Would this guy at least let her parents know so they could come back for her?

The hallway was very long and the sound of other dogs barking and crying rang loud in her ears. Her senses were hit with an overabundance of new sounds, smells, sights, and feelings all at once. She could smell the dogs, the food, people walking around her. Her paws stepped in wet puddles of urine that hadn't been cleaned up yet. The big, tall man holding the pole attached to her neck was walking so fast that she had trouble keeping up with him. She wanted to check everything out but he was tugging her along quickly to get to their destination. There was no time to sniff all the new things around her.

Slow down, Mister! she thought as she was dragged down the hallway. A loud voice came on over the intercom and it startled her. "Looking for a volunteer to do a stray dog walk-through. We have a young couple here who is looking for their lost dog." Ooh, maybe that was her parents coming back for her! Maybe they found out that the last man didn't want her anymore and realized that they had made a big mistake giving her away. After all, she had only been with him for a very short time, maybe a couple of weeks?

The big, tall man dragged her past a nice lady with a baggy full of treats and the lady stopped and gave her a treat.

She would have given her more if this guy would just slow down. What was his big rush anyway? Her neck was starting to hurt from the tension and pinching of the pole.

The man kept walking until they reached a closed door with a bunch of numbers on it. He swung open the door and the sound of other dogs came rushing at her so suddenly and loud, it made her ears hurt. The stench was potent. She started to cry a little bit out of fear and anxiety. She did not want to go into that loud, stinky room. She wasn't going to do it. She pulled back to try to stop him from going into the scary room, but it didn't work. She tried pressing her paws down on the ground and digging in as hard as she could to let him know she wasn't going any further. He wasn't her dad and she didn't have to listen to him. That didn't work either. She then plopped herself down onto the ground, her belly feeling the wet floor beneath her as she attempted to throw a tantrum right there in the hallway. The man just pulled harder on the pole, hurting her neck even more. The pads of her paws rubbed along the floor as he dragged her through the open doorway and into the hallway of the scary room. She thought she had found safety but now she wasn't sure she would survive this place.

She continued to resist going any further, but the man continued to drag her. Her paws burned from the friction of being pulled across the floor as she protested. He walked her past several dogs, and one of them lunged at her through the kennel door, rattling the door and startling her. Another dog was sleeping on the small cot that was placed in each kennel, appearing to be almost lifeless. She made eye contact with another dog who looked scared and was shivering in the back corner of his cage, before coming to an abrupt halt in front of an empty kennel.

The man finally stopped pulling her and lifted a latch to another door that led her into a very small, confined space where she would be staying while she was here. He pulled up on the pole, lifting her up in the air to avoid getting her paws caught on the bottom raised edge of the kennel, and he continued to tug her inside rather forcefully. Just as quickly as her last leg crossed the threshold to her new living space, the door slammed shut behind her and the big, tall man was gone.

Once again, she found herself alone and scared.

Friday

It was Friday morning and Brynn was running late, per usual. She rolled out of bed, threw on her normal Friday apparel, which consisted of Carhartt pants, a volunteer sweatshirt with a picture of a dog and the shelter's logo on it, some heavy-duty winter boots, and a bunch of other warm gear she tossed into her tote bag to take to the shelter with her.

She took a quick look at her reflection in the mirror and saw the very plain, low-maintenance girl she had come to be looking back at her. She rarely did anything special with her hair or wore much makeup, and she typically dressed in comfortable clothing or scrubs. Getting herself ready to go to the shelter was much like any other day for her. She pulled her hair back into a ponytail, brushed her teeth, and was ready to go. There was no reason to waste any time getting ready as she would soon smell of dogs and poop, while featuring mud, dog hair and poop on her clothing.

She quickly took her own three dogs outside to go potty before she left for the day. She gave them each a kiss and a few baby carrots for a little treat to tide them over until their dad got home from work. She told them each she loved them and that she was sorry she was leaving them again, but she had to go take care of the homeless dogs, like two of them once were themselves.

Brinkley, Molly, and Tino looked up at her with the most innocent eyes, pleading with her to stay home with them. They were the cutest dogs in the world to Brynn; one black pit bull mix, one white pit bull mix, and one old man golden retriever. It was so hard to resist crawling back into bed with them, but their eyes followed her all the way to the door as she exited the house. She was gone for the day.

Volunteering at Animal Control is not something Brynn took lightly. It's not like helping out at a doggy day care or a vet clinic, or even a humane society. It is hardcore and it is not for the weak-minded. You have to be strong both physically and mentally to be able to volunteer or work at a place like Animal Control. You have to be prepared to be dragged and pulled by some of the strongest dogs. You have to perfect your skills with leashing a dog who has been confined to a small space for 23 or more hours a day. You have to mentally be prepared for the worst to happen to these dogs, because one mistake or mess-up could mean life or death for that dog.

Brynn had seen it happen before; great dogs would come in and would mentally decline rapidly because they couldn't handle life in the shelter. It only takes one incident with a stressed-out dog for that dog to be determined too "unpredictable" or "unsafe" to adopt out to a member of the public. Sometimes it is admittedly the fault of the handler for doing something to trigger-stack the dog and increase their anxiety even more.

Trigger-stacking is a term used when referring to multiple stressful incidents occurring in a short time frame for an already stressed dog. For example, leashing a dog who is uncertain of the leash and taking that dog into a new room he is fearful of, only to meet a new male volunteer when that dog is fearful of men. This is trigger-stacking. One stressful incident immediately followed by another and yet another.

Other times, something the handler does *not* do may cause more anxiety for the dog. For example, not giving a new fearful dog the time he or she needs to make the decision to come out of their kennel when he or she is ready, could be detrimental to that dog's anxiety. Dogs are many times leashed and tugged out of their kennel when they are displaying body language that implies they aren't ready to come out yet. Either way, once the dog acts out and shows any form of aggression, that dog is likely not going to be deemed adoptable.

As a volunteer, it is important to be aware of the potential outcome for these dogs if mistakes are made. For this reason, and for the safety of the volunteers handling the dogs, they are required to take classes on canine body language and shadow a more seasoned volunteer before being approved to start working with the dogs.

The volunteers are also many times the bridge between a dog arriving at the shelter and an adopter coming through the doors to meet that dog. Between pictures, videos, bios, social media posts, relationships with local rescues, adoption events and fundraisers, etcetera, the volunteers are the backbone behind most adoptions that take place at Animal Control. Being able to see a dog through from its initial arrival at the shelter to its departure from the shelter to its forever home with its new family is one of the most rewarding parts of volunteering. It's what kept Brynn going back week after week.

Brynn walked through the door of the brick building like she did every Friday, which was her one day off from her job as a dental hygienist during the week. She drove about fifty minutes one way every week, because there was such a huge need for help here. She had found out about the need after adopting her own dog, Tino, from a local rescue. His foster mom was a volunteer here and Brynn thought she'd give it a try. It was a high-crime, inner-city shelter located in a big city that was well known for breeding pit bulls; it was not the uneventful small town she lived in, which up until recently was still considered a village. The need for help was substantial in comparison to her hometown's local shelter.

She walked inside and was instantly hit with the awful smells and cries of the nearly 120 dogs that were currently residing inside the building. She was used to it after volunteering here for five years, but the first step inside the door always kind of took her breath away for just a second. She made the long walk down the hallway to get to the volunteer locker room, listening to the heartbreaking cries, barks, and howls of all the dogs wanting out of their kennels. Some days she would have to make herself hold back tears at the initial sounds of desperation coming from the dogs.

Brynn entered the locker room, signed her name on the sign-in sheet, and stored her things in a locker. Already bundled up for the cold weather, she added gloves, a winter hat, and a neck warmer to her attire. She said hello to a few other volunteers she was used to seeing on Fridays, then stocked up her apron with milk bones, hot dog pieces, cow tails, poop bags, an air horn, and her phone.

She decided to start on the stray side of the building. One side of the building held strays who were on a stray hold for four to seven days, in hopes of their owners coming for them. The other side of the building was the adoption side. Once a stray completes the stray hold and is not claimed by its owner, it is evaluated by a shelter staff member and moved to the adoption side, making him or her available to be adopted into a new family. When the dog is evaluated, if the staff determines he or she is very reactive to other dogs, or is overly fearful or hyperactive, they will appropriately label the dog on the kennel card attached to the kennel. This way all volunteers and staff members are alerted to certain behaviors and/or concerns with the dog before taking the dog out of its kennel.

Brynn was making her way down one of the stray wards slowly that Friday morning. She had taken three dogs outside in about an hour's time, letting them go potty and run in the play yard for a bit. She usually tried to walk the dogs around the wood line of the property in addition to letting them run around in the play yard, if there was time to do so and enough volunteers were signed up for that day. Time didn't always allow for both a walk and playing in the fenced-in play yard, but today there were several volunteers, so ample time for both. She enjoyed days like this because it allowed her to spend more time getting to know the dogs since she wasn't so rushed.

After returning the last dog she had out to his kennel, she moved on to the next kennel. She put her clip with her name tag on the door and looked over the kennel card. No name and no info. This girl had just arrived the day before so had not yet been evaluated by staff.

"Well, hello, beautiful girl! My name is Brynn. Do you have a name?" Brynn smiled as the female dog looked curiously back at her with a tilted head, listening and trying to figure out what was about to happen. "Do you want to go outside with me? We can go for a walk, and I have some special treats just for you. If you're really good, I might even get you a big biscuit with some peanut butter on it when we come back inside."

Brynn laughed as the dog's head tilted to the opposite side, looking both confused and intrigued. "You are such a pretty girl! I bet you anything your family is out looking for you right now. Someone surely must be missing your sweet face."

Brynn saw a purple collar sitting in the basket attached

to her kennel, but there was no name or contact information for her owners. She rolled her eyes and the thought crossed her mind that there was a lot of stupidity in the world. A nameless collar with no information on it wasn't going to provide any information to the finder of a lost dog. But she quickly put that thought out of her mind, thinking maybe it was a new pet owner who didn't know any better yet. She had made similar mistakes with her own dogs at one time so she had to remind herself that not everyone was intellectually savvy when it came to caring for a dog.

When Brynn looked at the dog in front of her, the biggest brown eyes stared back at her through the prison-like bars of the kennel door. She was a medium-sized, all-black pit bull or pit mix. She couldn't have been much more than a year old. Her right ear was folded over on itself, and about a quarter of the tip of her left ear had been cropped. Her head remained tilted to the side as she looked back at Brynn with a curious but pleading gaze. Her right eye was a little lazy, wandering off to the side as her left eye looked straight ahead back at Brynn. She was perfectly imperfect.

Brynn knew as soon as she saw her that she was going to be special. Her tail started wagging so fast out of excitement to get out of that cage, and her butt moved from side to side along with the sway of her tail. "You're a little wiggle butt, I see!" Brynn laughed.

The nameless girl seemed a little hesitant when Brynn opened the kennel door to put the leash over her head. She sniffed the leash and looked up at Brynn with inquisitive eyes, not quite sure about the leash coming towards her head. She decided to take the risk, thinking anything would be better than sitting another minute in this cell. Brynn first tossed her some pieces of hot dog to win her trust, then proceeded to easily leash her. Brynn was unaware that the catch pole had been used on her the day before, hence why she was still a little leery of things being put around her neck.

The initial shyness didn't last long at all once they were outside. Brynn thought it must just be first-day nerves from being new to the shelter. She walked the new dog out to the big fenced-in play area, shut the gate behind her, and dropped the leash. As soon as she dropped the leash, the curious, excited girl ran around the play yard like she was finally free again. She ran all around the perimeter of the fenced-in area, taking advantage of every square inch of grass. She sniffed all around the edges of the yard. She kicked around a big red jolly ball that had been left in the play area. She got the zoomies. She rolled on her back to feel the grass beneath her coat, her paws in the air as she scooted herself from side to side to really feel the blades of grass on her back.

The cold air felt so good on her face after being cooped up inside of that smelly, stuffy cage for the last 24 hours. It felt so good to be able to relieve herself without worrying about getting in trouble for going potty inside, even though no one ever came to let her outside until now…*rude*, she thought to herself. The nice girl who brought her out threw a tennis ball for her to chase and rewarded her with treats when she showed her she knew how to sit pretty. Her mom had taught her that trick, so she was able to impress Brynn and earn all kinds of yummy treats by showing off her skills. She knew the commands *sit, shake,* and *lay down*, all thanks to her mom.

The sweet, silly young girl sat down on a bench next to Brynn and received all kinds of affection, gentle petting, and scratches behind her ears. It felt so good to feel loved again. She couldn't help but jump onto Brynn's lap and kiss her all over her face in appreciation. Her kisses made Brynn laugh, so she didn't stop.

She was grateful to have someone to love again, but she really missed her family and still hoped they would be coming for her.

January 2021
(Several Months Earlier)

B rynn arrived at the shelter around 12:00 pm and planned to stay until closing time, which was 6:00 pm. She knew they were short on volunteers today and they had just brought in a big group of dogs who were involved in a dog fighting bust. It's like they say, "when it rains, it pours."

This group of dogs was considered police custody since they were technically "evidence" in the abuse case. When this happened, the police custody dogs were stuck at Animal Control until the court case was over, or until the defendant surrendered their dogs to Animal Control. Unfortunately for the dogs, this sometimes dragged on for several months or even years.

Brynn knew it was going to be a long, busy day with the additional new dogs and fewer volunteers signed up to help. It was blustery outside. The wind was biting and there was still quite a bit of snow on the ground from a recent winter storm. It wasn't unusual for some volunteers to stop coming in during the winter months, and it wasn't unusual for fewer adoptions to take place during the winter months. Michigan winters could be dreadful some days, but these dogs still needed to get outside for some fresh air and to be able to relieve themselves. Even if it was sometimes only 10 minutes a day, it gave them a small amount of excitement to look forward to each day, some free time to break up the boredom and frustration of sitting in their kennels.

Brynn opened the door to the ward that was labeled "police hold dogs." She wasn't sure what to expect, given these dogs had come from a fighting ring. Would they be mean? Aggressive? Scared? She was about to find out, as she was the only one walking dogs for the first few hours of her shift, and none of these dogs had been taken out yet. Sometimes Brynn's lack of fear towards some of these dogs worried her, but she always gave the dogs the benefit of the doubt before coming to any conclusions about them. They all deserved a chance.

This group had been at Animal Control for about five days now, and someone had given them names. She wasn't sure if they came in with names or not, but she suspected the staff had named them upon arrival. They would soon collectively be known as the "beer dogs." Reading the names on the kennel cards as she walked up and down the row, she read off:

Shandy
Guinness
Blondie
Porter
Killian
Brewski
Brogan
Donelly
Tula
Milwaukee

She had heard there were others who had already been put into foster homes, some being young puppies who the shelter always tried to find foster homes for. The thought is that no puppy should have to grow up unsocialized in the shelter environment. Most of the time, it is easier to find a foster placement for a puppy than an adult dog.

Brynn noticed many of these dogs seemed to be quite hyperactive in their kennels, very stressed, barking, drooling; one of them was jumping off the sides of the kennel walls as if he was attempting to parkour. Some had obvious scars on their faces and bodies. Others did not. Some were emaciated. Some were not.

A few of them seemed intimidating, but she reminded herself that barrier frustration was a real thing, because it was. She had seen it so many times…a dog going crazy inside of the kennel, only to calm right down as soon as she cracked open the door to put the leash on. Eliminating that barrier of the kennel door was all that was needed for some dogs to completely show a shift in behavior.

She decided to start with the boy named Donelly.

Holy crap, this dog is nuts! What am I doing? He was all over his kennel, jumping, barking, and climbing the walls. After taking a few minutes to leash him, Brynn and Donelly walked outside. He didn't seem to want much to do with her, other than using her as a body to jump off of. She took a head bunt to the face at least two times from his constant jumping. She tried to harness him with her long leash to take him for a walk but was not successful. He continued to jump up aimlessly and squirm around, making it nearly impossible to safely wrap her leash around his body to harness him. He seemed like he didn't really know how to be a dog. Not affectionate at all. Zero manners. Without a doubt had never been walked on a leash. He seemed to be kind of aloof once he settled down. He wasn't interested in pets from Brynn or sitting close to her, so she gave him his space and let him explore everything on his own. He continuously jumped up at her and was biting at the sleeves of her coat as she walked him back inside.

That was interesting, she thought after returning him to his kennel.

One down…

Next up was Blondie. This poor little girl was covered in scars. She had clearly not lived a good life. She was skinny, her ribs visible. She had blondish-tan-colored hair and a weathered look to her. She was as sweet as could be. The only thing she wanted was to be loved. She laid next to Brynn the entire time she was outside, enjoying the gentle pets and her belly being rubbed. Brynn immediately thought of her own dog, Molly. They were so similar in their loving personalities and desire for affection. This poor girl had probably never experienced any affection before coming here. Sadly, being at Animal Control is many times the best life some of these dogs have ever experienced. They are fed, loved, protected from harm, and given shelter, which is more than a lot of them have ever had. This girl was likely used as a bait dog based on the several scars on her face and body.

It broke Brynn's heart to imagine such a sweet girl being

beat up by other dogs at the command of her owner. She must have been so scared and confused, not having anyone around to protect her from harm. Blondie was an absolute doll who Brynn could have spent all day with if there was time. She immediately stole Brynn's heart.

Killian was next. He was what they referred to as a "leash biter." He was very jumpy and constantly biting at the leash. Once outside he was a great boy with a friendly person-ality, and he enjoyed running around in the play area. After wearing himself out from running and playing, he sat in front of Brynn with a big smile, awaiting her pets. Getting Killian leashed to go outside and getting the leash off to go back inside was tricky because of his constant habit of biting at the leash. If you weren't careful, your hand could easily get in the way and get bitten. Brynn would be sure to note this on his kennel card so that proper precautions would be taken by the next person to get him out. Poor guy was so stressed out.

She walked up to the next kennel, Brewski. Brewski was a big boy, a black-and-white pit bull. He cowered in the back corner of his kennel, tail tucked, ears pinned back, big wide eyes, terrified. Brynn tossed him some treats and he slowly came forward for the treats, but then retreated to his corner. He was always keeping his eyes on her but never looking directly at her. She could tell he wanted to come out, but he wasn't so sure about her yet. She tossed him some hot dog pieces and would come back for him later to try again. She didn't want to push it if he was that scared.

Brynn proceeded to take out the remaining "beer dogs" before returning to Brewski. She saw more stressed-out, hyperactive, starved-for-attention dogs. Dogs who didn't know how to "dog," if you will. Many were very thin with scars from fighting, yet they seemed like friendly dogs overall. They were such forgiving animals; it was truly amazing to her since they had clearly been through hell before getting to this point. Whoever could do this to these animals was a monster, in her opinion. She was thankful these dogs ended up here so they would at least be safe from any more abuse.

Last but not least, she returned to Brewski. "Let's try this again, big guy. I know you want to come outside with me, don't you?" She knelt down to his level and spoke gently in a quiet, calm tone so as not to startle him. She tossed some more pieces of hot dogs and he slowly came closer to the door, grabbed the hot dogs, then ran back to his corner where he felt safe. His eyes were fearful yet curious.

She laid the leash on the ground in front of her in a big loop and placed some hot dog pieces inside the loop; it was the oldest trick in the book. And it worked. Each time he approached the loop to grab his treats, Brynn would slowly and carefully lift the leash a little closer to his head, until finally he was comfortable to hang around long enough for her to loop it all the way around his neck while he ate the yummy treats laid out for him. Brynn was able to lift the loop over his head and slowly tighten the leash while lightly petting below his chin.

At that point Brewski seemed relieved. It was a stressful situation for him, but he really wanted to trust her so that he could go outside. Brewski walked nicely next to Brynn as they walked outside. Every few steps he would cautiously look up at her as if he was looking for reassurance that he was going to be okay in this place.

The cold air hit his face immediately and he jumped at the sound of the nearby flag hitting the pole from the wind. He was easily startled, very alert to his surroundings. Brynn continued to walk slowly and gently with him, so as not to startle him. He sat down next to Brynn when she took him into the fenced-in area. She was sitting on a bench, letting him choose what he wanted to do.

As he sat next to her, she took note of his big black head with a white stripe down the center of his face and around his nose. He had white on his chest, belly, and the tips of his toes. The white on his chest and belly was dirty. His brown eyes appeared to be worried, as if he wasn't sure what was happening. His brows were furrowed and his forehead wrinkled. Brynn tried to reassure him that he was safe here and he was going to be fine, telling him we would take good care of him. He cautiously climbed his front legs up onto her lap as she continued to gently pet him and talk to him, occasionally glancing over at her as if he was listening.

She was slowly gaining his trust…

Brewski

Week after week, Brynn got to know Brewski a little bit better. She looked forward to taking him out first when she got to the shelter and always hoped that no one else had gotten to him yet. She felt too guilty taking out a dog who had already been out that day, when there were so many other dogs still needing to get outside for the first time. The one thing working in her favor was the fact that Brewski wouldn't come out of his kennel for every volunteer. He had his quirks, and one of them was his shyness.

He was a bashful boy who was leery of a lot of people, understandably so, given his history. For many volunteers he would still cower in the back of his kennel and sometimes pace back and forth out of uncertainty. But he trusted Brynn and each week he came to her a little quicker to get that leash on. She would take him outside and take him for long walks along the wood line so he could sniff and explore all that he wanted. They would sit on the bench together while she stroked his dirty black-and-white coat and told him that someday he was going to be in the best home with a wonderful family to love and spoil him. This place was only a moment in time so she would help him to make the most of it while he was here. He seemed to listen to her. The expression on his face was always very serious, as if he wasn't sure how to relax or have fun. His eyebrows were usually creased with worry and he rarely smiled. He was an old, gentle soul in a big, youthful pit bull's body. He had the most troubled yet kind brown eyes.

Sometimes Brynn would look into his eyes and wonder what he was thinking, or what kind of hell he had lived through prior to coming to Animal Control. Had he been trained to fight his fellow dog friends? Had he been used as a bait dog? Was he chained up to a fence in the back yard 24/7? Had he ever been shown any affection at all? Her heart broke at the thought of his past. His eyes told a story that only he knew, and she wished he could tell it to her so she could try to help him find some peace.

One Friday Brynn had planned a day trip for Brewski. The shelter allowed volunteers to take a dog out for the day to give them a break and to see how they do outside of the shelter environment. Many times, just putting an "adopt me" bright-colored vest on the dog would draw enough attention to start a conversation with a member of the public about the dog, and to recommend that they come to Animal Control to meet some of their fabulous dogs. But with Brewski being a police custody dog, he wasn't adoptable until the case was resolved, so there was no such vest for Brewski. Just a fun day out filled with adventures and new things for him to explore.

Brynn went into the shelter to pick up Brewski, who she was now referring to as her boyfriend because there was definitely a love connection there. She approached his kennel and said, "Brewski, are you ready to get out of this place and have some fun?" This time he came right up to the door as she unlatched it and cracked it open to leash him. She wrapped the leash around his body in order to harness him for better control, since she planned on taking him to some nice, long walking trails at the local park. It was a beautiful spring day in early April and this boy deserved a fun-filled day away from that dark, lonely kennel he had already been in for three months.

She walked Brewski out to her car in the parking lot and right away, there was a problem. Brewski was afraid of her car. He wouldn't get in it. She tossed hot dog pieces and milk bones into the back seat of her car, and neither seemed to work. He was refusing to come close and he kept the leash pulled taut at its longest stretch. Brynn crouched down to the ground and called him over. He reluctantly came closer to her and allowed her to pet the sides of his face, but any movement towards standing up or motioning him to the car, and he ran back to the end of the leash. This poor boy had likely never ridden inside a vehicle, aside from the scary van that seized him from his home and brought him to this place. Brynn would have to try something else to lure him in. She did not want this to be a traumatic experience for him. He needed to know that car rides could be associated with fun times and good things. She handed Brewski off to another volunteer and went back inside the building to load up a big milk bone with some peanut butter.

When she returned to the car and put the desirable treat on her back seat, he raised his nose up in the air and sniffed as if he wanted a taste of that yummy peanut butter. His eyes looked to Brynn as he sniffed and thought about it. But he wouldn't budge, even for peanut butter. Brynn handed Brewski off again and proceeded to climb into the back seat herself. She called for Brewski from her back seat and he looked curious. She tossed hot dog pieces out the door onto the ground and he ate them, lifting his head up to investigate what exactly was going on inside of this thing. She then held her hand out with the peanut butter milk bone and called for him. He approached her hand and began licking the peanut butter from the milk bone, as Brynn slowly pulled the treat farther away from him to lure him inside.

He climbed his front legs up onto the back seat of her car and looked around. She kept calling for him to encourage him, but he seemed hesitant and a little confused about what he was supposed to do. The other volunteer slowly started to pet his side and then his backside while talking to him, and then carefully lifted his rear end up to help him jump into the back seat.

Just like that, he was in the car! It took some time, but he was now sitting in the backseat of Brynn's car, ready for their day out together. She had put a comfortable blanket and pillow in the back, just in case he wanted to rest his cute, big head during the ride. She wanted this boy to experience all of life's good things and she would try her best to show him what life had to offer outside of dog fights and animal shelters.

Brewski stayed in the back seat during the fifteen-minute drive to the park. He didn't move around too much but was curiously looking through the windows. When they arrived at the park, he jumped out of the car with ease. The thought of getting him back into the car hadn't crossed Brynn's mind until now, but she wouldn't worry about it until that time came.

Brynn and Brewski walked and walked, and then they walked some more. It was a beautiful sunny day and this park had countless trails to choose from. Much of it was shaded, which was nice for Brewski so he didn't overheat. There was a nice, calming stream that ran through the park; you could hear the water trickling and the birds chirping. The grass was newly green as spring had recently made its arrival. Some of the tulips and daffodils were just starting to bloom. Brynn and Brewski would occasionally stop and sit under a tree, drink some water, and take a break from walking. Brewski was content sitting under a tree and taking in his surroundings.

Brynn took pictures of their "date" to send to her husband and her friends at the shelter. She texted a selfie of her and Brewski to another volunteer who claimed he was *her* boyfriend, with the words "he loves me more." She laughed to herself as she hit send.

Brewski was a great walking partner. He didn't pull too hard for his size and he kept up with Brynn's pace. He would sniff around in the grass from time to time and then come right back to Brynn's side. Brynn knew he was a great boy, but she never imagined he would be *this* great! They passed other walkers, bikers, joggers, and even other dogs during their walk. Brewski didn't pay attention to any of them. Not a peep came from him. He was the perfect gentleman, and she couldn't get over how well he was doing.

After walking and relaxing in the shade off and on for close to two hours, Brynn decided to head back to the car. *Please God, let him get into my car.* She opened the door to the backseat of her car, and Brewski froze. She climbed right in while holding his leash, and with just a little encouragement, Brewski followed her inside. He was making such progress with all these new experiences today. He was beginning to show potential to make a great family pet some day, once he was released from his court case and became adoptable. She was so proud of him, she could cry.

They listened to some calming smooth jazz on the way back to the shelter. Brynn could see Brewski in her rear-view mirror. He would stand up about halfway to look out the window and then lay back down, unsure if he should be standing while driving. He struck her as the type to be all about safety and following the rules, always being cautious. He did this half-stand thing several times but always resorted back to lying down on the blanket with a slightly worried look in his eyes. He didn't know she was watching him and smiling.

Brynn pulled into a McDonald's and ordered a plain cheeseburger and a small French fry. They sat in the parking lot of McDonald's and shared their meal. She would pull off little bites of cheeseburger for Brewski and his eyes would get really big and he would eat it up as fast as he could. He had a few fries but his preference was definitely the cheeseburger. He had never tasted anything so delicious before in his life.

When they pulled back into the parking lot of the shelter, Brynn sadly said, "It's time to go back now, Brewski. I sure hope you had fun today, buddy. I had a blast with you and I can't wait to do it again." He looked back at her with perked-up ears and kind eyes. She walked him around in the grass for a minute to see if he had to go potty before going inside.

As she proceeded to walk towards the building, Brewski put the brakes on. He froze in place and would not move any closer. He didn't want to go back into that building. He had no idea when the next time he would get to go outside would be. It broke Brynn's heart. If she could take him home with her, she would do it in a heartbeat. She knew that two of her dogs would be a lot of energy for Brewski, and her senior dog's health was starting to decline, so it wouldn't be fair to him either. She also knew her husband would never be able to successfully foster a dog and not keep it forever.

His heart for dogs was as big as hers and he would without a doubt fall hard for Brewski and want to adopt him after his court case was resolved. Brynn was not looking to add a fourth dog to their clan.

After about ten minutes of bribing Brewski inside with every treat imaginable, she gave up on treats. "Brewski, you are way too big for me to carry you inside! You're going to hurt my back and then I won't even be able to come take you for walks and cheeseburgers."

Still nothing. He just looked back at her with those eyes that carried so much emotion, as if to say, *please don't make me go back.* His paws were cemented into the ground and he wasn't moving. Brynn decided she was going to have to carry him inside. She crouched down and used all her leg strength to lift this guy up and carry him inside to his kennel. He was easily sixty-plus pounds and her lower back wasn't happy about this decision, but she didn't know what other option she had. No one else had been outside to ask for help, so she just went for it.

Little did she realize that this would be the method of returning Brewski to his kennel for the next several months to come. And he would soon learn to expect nothing less.

And Then There Were Two

As the weeks turned into months, Brewski sat in his nine-by-four-feet kennel day after day. The days seemed endless to Brewski, but he was used to the boredom, given his previous life of being chained to a fence. Some days he would lay on his cot and barely move for hours. He tried to hold his potty but realistically, it wasn't possible most days. His own feces sometimes surrounded his cot until a staff member got to his ward for cleaning. His only glimmer of excitement was his short time outside with his volunteer friends.

The seasons were changing. Spring quickly turned to summer and summer to fall, and now it was winter once again. He had arrived in January and Christmas was now approaching. As the court case involving Brewski and the other "beer dogs" was still pending, the dogs continued to live in the shelter. Once the court case was resolved, the dogs would be released to Animal Control and made available for adoption.

Brewski continued to be his worried, cautious self, but he learned to trust more people the longer he was at Animal Control. There was a handful of volunteers who were able to take him out now, and some that he still wasn't comfortable with and wouldn't even approach. It wasn't unusual to see Brewski's big ole body hanging in the arms of a volunteer because he wouldn't go back inside the building willingly. He always had this sad, pathetic look on his face as he was being carried back inside. It was sad but also kind of adorable to see. The volunteers came to expect this out of him as he had been at Animal Control for so long; he was a well-known face among everyone.

When Brewski was outside, he gained so much confidence. He was learning to play with the big jolly balls outside and run the fence with other dogs, slowly becoming a dog for the first time in his life. Brynn took him a few different times to get another cheeseburger and a pup cup from the local coffee shop, just to give him a break from the shelter from time to time. The ladies working the drive-thru at the coffee shop would inquire about Brewski and load up his pup cup after hearing his story. If his eyes got big for the cheeseburger, they practically doubled in size the first time he experienced a pup cup full of whipped cream and garnished with special treats. He had never tasted so many delicious treats in his life. Brewski loved Brynn and she absolutely adored him.

Brynn was amazed by his transformation from when he first came to Animal Control. He was now showing so much more confidence overall, and he even smiled often, showing her that he was able to relax more. Inside the building he was much more fearful and hesitant. He wouldn't walk into most rooms inside the shelter. Whenever anyone tried to take him into a smaller, quiet room to spend some time with him, he would put the brakes on outside the door and refuse to enter. This was something they would continue to work on with him during his stay, to try to relieve some of his anxiety about these inside rooms. Brynn wondered what had happened to him to trigger these fears. If only Brewski could tell them what he was afraid of, they could try to help him work through it.

One day Brynn was carrying Brewski back inside to return him to his kennel, his feet and belly hanging from her arms as they walked down the halls. He had not wanted to come inside and was not happy with Brynn. She sat him down on the floor of his kennel and he looked up at her with such sad eyes. He lightly whimpered and pushed his muzzle into her arm to ask for more pets. With one hand on each cheek, she held his big head in her hands and looked him straight in the eyes, her thumbs gently stroking his cheeks. After petting him some more, she stood up, closed the latch to his door, and said, "Oh buddy, I know. I love you so much. Things will get better for you, I promise."

She had tears in her eyes as she walked away. His sad eyes followed her all the way to the doorway at the end of the hall. She had known Brewski for almost a year now and he had taught her so much. He was so resilient, forgiving, accepting, brave...she was so proud of him. He displayed characteristics that she struggled to attain herself. It was truly amazing how far he had come after being treated so poorly by humans. She wished she had half the courage he had.

Brynn walked across the hall to the volunteer locker room to wipe away her tears and take a moment to collect herself. She didn't want anyone to see her and think something was wrong. Sometimes she just had moments like this, when this place really got to her. After a few minutes had passed, she heard some commotion in the hallway and a male voice saying firmly, "Get down!"

In walked Derrick, another volunteer who walked dogs with her on Fridays. He appeared a little frazzled. "Have you met Piper yet, Brynn?" At the other end of Derrick's leash stood the young black little pit bull she had walked on the stray side a couple of weeks prior. She wondered what had happened to her or if she had been picked up by her owners. It only took her a second to realize it was her. Those big brown eyes were unforgettable.

"Yes, I have! Oh my gosh, hello again, Miss Piper! I know you, silly girl. And I love your new name! I'm so happy I get to see you again!" Brynn's sadness quickly turned into a smile as she bent down to pet Piper.

Derrick told Brynn that Piper was quite the wild child coming out of her kennel, and to be prepared if she ever took her out. Apparently, Piper had picked up some bad manners over the last two weeks and liked to barge out of her kennel full force once the door to her kennel opened. She would jump up almost as high as your face, so you had to dodge your head to avoid a head bunt. Then she would grab onto the leash and try to walk you rather than you walk her. She was a take-charge kind of gal and was lacking patience.

But sitting in front of Brynn was the sweetest, silliest little girl just wanting to be petted and loved on. She had just given Derrick a run for his money in the hallway before he had brought her into the locker room. Now she sat in front of Brynn with a smirk on her face that would soon become one of her trademark expressions. Lips pulled back on one side of her face only, as if she had just done something naughty and was quite proud of herself for doing it. Oh boy, she was going to be a handful, this one; full of piss and vinegar without a doubt.

Brynn and Derrick sat down on the bench in the locker room and Piper sat in front of them just soaking up all their love and attention. Her body leaned into Brynn and she whimpered and moaned softly as Brynn scratched all the right spots. She eventually plopped herself down on the ground and rolled over onto her back as if to ask for a belly rub. She was really turning up the charm for them. How could anyone resist this sweet, sassy girl? And what was her story? Brynn had hoped her owners had come for her but after being here two weeks, the chances were slim that they'd still be coming.

"Yeah, I've walked her three days in a row now," Derrick continued. "She's a handful, but she's the sweetest dog I think I've ever met. She just needs to learn to calm down after being so amped up in her kennel. I think she'll make a great companion for someone with a little training though. She's definitely my favorite girl here right now. Aren't you, Piper?" Derrick reached down and scratched her belly as Piper ate up all the attention.

Later that same day, Brynn decided to get Piper out again herself. She had loved that girl when she first met her as a stray and she wanted to spend more time with her. Derrick was right; she brought the thunder coming out of her kennel and she immediately grabbed that leash as if to say, *Come on, let's go!* She wasn't the most patient girl, but as long as you were ready for her, it really wasn't too much of an issue.

When they entered the fenced-in area outdoors, Brynn dropped the leash and Piper took off running. She had the zoomies and was pushing her head into the snow mounds as if she were bobbing for apples in the snow. She ran in circles until she was exhausted, then came over to Brynn and jumped up on the bench next to her, panting after having so much fun. "Are you all done acting a fool, Piper?" Brynn laughed as she brushed the white snowflakes off her black coat with her gloved hand.

She couldn't believe how much Piper enjoyed playing in the snow. A trail of her paw prints left a complex maze in the snow from her endless running and playing. She was such a silly girl with what seemed like never-ending energy. She entertained herself with the various toys and balls that were out there, and any time another volunteer walked a dog by the fence, it sparked her interest as she wanted so badly to play with them. Her ears would perk up, one of them always folded over and the other one cropped like someone had taken a pair of scissors to the tip of it. Her head would tilt out of curiosity and then she would start running along the fence, crying, as if to say, *Come run with me!*

She was the opposite of Brewski. She had confidence for days, immediately loved you without having to gain your trust, and had not a fear in the world. She was always smiling with a goofy expression on her face, one eye drifting off to the side and her tongue hanging out. When she'd get sassy, her trademark smirk would make an appearance because she knew exactly what she was doing. This girl was amazing. She had the biggest personality. Brynn couldn't help but smile when she looked at her.

After taking advantage of every second of her time outside, Piper was clearly exhausted. Brynn took her back inside into one of the quiet rooms and Piper laid across her lap as Brynn rubbed her belly and scratched behind her ears. She had worn herself out and now was being a stage-five clinger. Brynn took several cute pictures of Piper and some selfies with her to use on social media to promote her to get adopted. She couldn't imagine it would take very long for this girl to get snatched up, as she was basically perfect, in Brynn's eyes. She was the full package: adorable, smart, silly, playful, loving, cuddly...what more could anyone want?

Brynn couldn't bring herself to put Piper back in her kennel because she was enjoying herself so much, but eventually she had to return her. Brynn wondered how anyone could have such a special girl and not come looking for her when she went missing. What was wrong with people? Her heart broke a little bit more every time she fell hard for a dog. Every dog had to have a story...a beginning that somehow brought them to this place. She wondered, what was Piper's story?

The thought of her own dogs ending up in a place like this gave her so much anxiety. They were her family, her kids...how could so many people just not come looking for their family member? This was something she would never be able to understand.

She did know one thing, though...she was going to make it her mission to find both Piper and Brewski the very best homes with the very best families. That was a promise she made to herself and to them.

Nine by Four

Nine feet by four feet. That was the size of each dog's kennel at Animal Control. Sometimes, many times, in fact, when the count was high and the shelter ran out of room to house more dogs, each kennel had a hidden door that could be dropped down through the center to split it into two separate kennels. They would then refer to that particular kennel as having an "A" side and a "B" side. If the dog was lucky, it would be on the "A" side because it was slightly larger than the "B" side. Dogs on the "B" side many times were lying in their own urine and feces because there was literally no room to escape it. The living conditions were rough at times, but it was that or these dogs would be living on the streets. They were at least safe here with food, water, and shelter.

Brynn had to remind herself of this often in order not to feel too frustrated with the place she was volunteering for. She reminded herself that the reason she was here was *because* there was such a big need for help. The staff worked their hardest to keep the kennels clean, but this was a county-run facility. It was often understaffed, and the dogs just kept coming in every single day. For every dog that was adopted, it seemed like two or more replaced it the following day. It was a never-ending cycle of backyard breeding and irresponsible pet owners.

The staff did their best to ensure these dogs were safe. Were conditions ideal? Probably not. But it was meant to be a temporary living space for the dogs until they could get adopted into a new home. Dogs weren't supposed to live here for six months, or a year, or more. Unfortunately, they sometimes did. A dog like Brewski, who was held up in a court case and would be here for an undetermined amount of time, would most likely be guaranteed a full-size kennel. Piper, on the other hand, had to earn a full-size kennel. And that she did…

It was 6:00 pm and the lights were shut off for the day. Piper sat in her kennel looking at the wall. She hadn't been outside since about 11:00 am that morning and she really had to pee. But she knew what it meant when the lights went out. It would be at least another sixteen hours before she would see any people walking around in here again.

People started showing up around 10:00-ish each morning. She was on the "A" side of her kennel…she was considered lucky. How this was luck, she had no idea. She had originally had the full kennel to herself, but earlier that afternoon, a couple of shelter staff members had walked inside the ward she was in and put down the partition in her kennel. She could hear the door closing and latching on the other side of the room. She then heard them talking about how awful people could be, and how cruel it was to do this to a senior with health problems. She wasn't sure what that was all about, but she decided to lie down in her now-very-small living space and try to fall asleep to make the time pass faster.

She struggled to get comfortable and kept standing up on her small cot to turn herself around to find the best spot. After circling in place a few times, she curled up into a ball and tried to fall asleep, but she couldn't. Her eyes were open and even though she couldn't see much in the darkness, she knew the only thing she was missing seeing was the wall. If she turned to her right, she would see another wall. If she looked up to the sky, she would see the ceiling. She was surrounded by walls in this confined space that felt like a cell to her. She couldn't help but wonder why she was being punished. Her mom used to let her sleep in bed with her, and Piper would curl up in the nook of her legs, or sometimes she would burrow under the covers to keep warm next to her dad's feet. During the daytime she had a bed of her own on the floor in the living room and the sunlight would come in through the big picture window and shine on her face. There was no sunlight in this place.

She always got to go potty outside right before bed and again when she woke up in the morning, when she lived in her old home. None of this holding it for twenty-three (or more) hours a day nonsense. This place was like torture. She had to pee so bad! *Somebody let me out of here before I explode!* she thought to herself.

It was dark, cold, and she swore they found the most uncomfortable cot for her to sleep on. She didn't consider herself to be high-maintenance but dang, can't a girl get an actual bed to sleep on? At least give her a blanket to provide some warmth and comfort. She had heard a rumor that some dogs try to destroy or eat the blankets, which was the reason why they couldn't have them in their kennel. The same went for toys. It was just the uncomfortable cot and the walls surrounding her.

She thought for a moment that she might be going crazy. Was this really happening, or was it all some kind of sick nightmare? Piper stood up again in the dark and this time she began to cry. She started to pace around her small living space as she cried. She just wanted to get out of this kennel so bad; she was getting more and more frustrated. Having to pee wasn't helping matters at all. Her "cellmate" over on the "B" side must have heard her because he started to whine and then bark at her through the door that separated them from each other. She stood closer to the dividing partition and barked lightly back at him, her head tilted in curiosity. They continued to communicate with each other this way until others in the ward started to wake up and cry or bark. The recently quiet ward was now loud and unruly, and Piper was to blame. So much for making friends here.

Amid all the excitement, Piper accidentally relieved herself as she just couldn't hold it anymore. She was embarrassed and ashamed. She found a corner that wasn't covered in urine to curl up in and tried to fall asleep again.

Down the hall in a different ward was Brewski. He had a larger kennel so he was able to walk around and stretch his legs if he got antsy. He lay peacefully on his cot and lightly snored. Brewski appreciated the quiet at night and was usually able to sleep fairly well. He came from an abusive, neglectful home and had been next in line to be trained in the business of dog fighting. He was young and that had worked to his advantage. He hadn't actually been introduced to the fighting yet, but he witnessed it every day. He watched as his friends were put through hell in order to please their owners and avoid getting beaten. He tried to comfort them when their bodies were all torn up and they were in pain, or when they were forced to attack their own friends. He would lick their wounds when given an opportunity, and listen to them all night long as they cried in physical pain or mental anguish.

He had known his time was coming soon and he was terrified. He hadn't experienced the fighting side of things yet, but he had been neglected most days and was hit or kicked if he did anything to displease his owners. So being in this place really wasn't so bad for him. There were days he would get bored being stuck inside all day, but he was always hopeful that one of his volunteer friends would come for him. He was making new friends here and his belly was usually full. He knew that he would be safe here.

He often thought about Blondie, one of his closest friends from his previous home. He wondered how she was doing and if she was here. While he slept on his cot, his paws began to twitch and his teeth began to chatter as he had nightmares about watching his old friends being tortured in front of his eyes. His inability to help them made him feel so powerless. These nightmares were a usual occurrence for Brewski.

Some time had passed when Piper opened her eyes, maybe a few hours? It was still pretty dark, so it was hard to tell exactly what time it was, but her stomach was beginning to growl and it seemed as if the darkness had ever so slightly lifted.

Piper woke up to find herself scrunched up into a corner of her kennel; her legs and hips felt stiff and achy. *Oh, that's right,* she thought as she stood up and felt the sticky, dried-up urine under her paws. She rolled her eyes as she remembered where she was…it was every man for himself in this dreadful place she had grown to hate. She was humiliated about the pee, but she also realized that no one here really seemed to care but her. She certainly wouldn't be getting into trouble for having an accident here. These people seemed to *expect* it, much unlike her previous homes. Half the time the staff members here would hose down her kennel with her still in it, which she found to be quite rude, but at least it was getting cleaned.

She heard a sound across the partition coming from her roommate. Crying, it sounded like. It was a soft, very sad and desperate cry. He must have been trying to be quiet so that no one else heard him. But Piper heard. The two dogs were practically cuddled up next to each other with only the barrier of the partition separating them. Piper had spotted a very small gap between the partition and the adjacent wall way up high towards the top of her kennel, that she could only reach if she stood up on her hind legs. She stood up and pushed her eye up to the hole, standing tall with her hind legs stretched out and her front paws placed against the wall that separated them.

Looking down, she could see the source of the crying. He appeared to be another pit bull like herself, on the smaller side, though. He must have had an accident in the night too, because he had feces smeared all over his kennel. It was everywhere…the ground, the walls, in his hair and on his paws…everywhere. Maybe he wasn't feeling well or he ate too much. She thought she would probably be crying too if she had to sleep in that filth.

The sad dog looked up at her with tear-filled, worried eyes. He looked old. His face was white and his body looked frail and weathered, almost sickly. His eyes told her he was terrified. Piper stared back into his eyes and felt helpless. She wanted to help him but didn't know how. To be honest, he had just arrived yesterday and she was kind of annoyed with him because he took the other half of her kennel from her. Now she felt guilty for feeling that way.

She lightly cried back at the old man and her one eye exuded kindness and compassion through the gap in the wall, as if to say, *I'm here for you if you need anything. I'm in the same boat, but I've been here a bit longer and I know the ropes if you have any questions. It will get better. I won't lie, it's not fun here, but it will get better.* The two held their gaze for a few minutes. Then she lowered herself back down to the ground and sat in silence, hearing only the low cries of her new friend next door.

It seemed like hours went by before the crying finally stopped. He must have fallen asleep. Piper was feeling somewhat defeated. Would she ever get out of this depressing place again, or was this it for her? Would she have to occupy herself for hours upon hours every day in this tiny cell for the rest of her life, staring at the walls in front of her while listening to old dogs cry? Would she grow old herself in this very kennel, turning white in the face with her health ailing like her new friend? Her heart started to race as she was getting anxious thinking about it. She was hungry but knew it would still be a while before breakfast came around. The only thing she could do until then was to sit and wait some more, and maybe go back to sleep to pass the time. She hoped with every fiber in her body that someone would take her outside at a decent time today, or she thought she just might lose her mind on the "A" side of this suite.

Piper meets Brewski

Brewski heard footsteps walking down the hall of his ward, and he immediately jumped up from the cot he'd been lying on for what felt like days to investigate what was going on. As the footsteps grew closer, he realized it was his volunteer friend, Brynn! She approached his kennel, clipped her name tag to his kennel door, and opened the latch on the door to leash him. He was so excited to go outside that he forgot for a moment that he was scared of walking by some of the bigger, louder dogs in his row. He sped down the ward next to Brynn as the dogs barked and lunged toward him from inside their kennels.

When Brynn opened the door that led them outside, Brewski immediately lifted his leg to pee on the brick wall of the building. Sometimes he held it so long that his stomach started to hurt, but he just didn't feel right about going inside.

He wasn't supposed to go potty inside of his kennel at his old house, but some days the two men didn't come to the house until very late at night and he had no choice. Finding accidents in the dogs' kennels would always send the two men into an outrage, and it would result in a beating for Brewski and the other dogs. The men would usually let a small group of dogs out at a time to go potty, in two separate fenced-in areas in the back yard. This was the only chance Brewski had to interact physically with the other dogs. Most of his time was spent chained up in the front yard where he was pretty much isolated from the other dogs. When he was on a chain outside, he could go potty any time; when inside his kennel in the house, he wouldn't dare.

So Brewski tried to always hold his potty in his kennel here at the shelter, unless it was an emergency. Unfortunately, there were more emergencies than he'd like to admit. He felt so embarrassed when his volunteer friends came to take him out if they saw he left a mess in his kennel. He tried his best...it was all he could do.

Brynn walked Brewski around the premises for a while. They walked along the edge of the woods, stopping often for Brewski to sniff and investigate. They sat on the curb to the paved parking lot and watched the other dogs walking and playing. Brewski enjoyed sitting in the sun, taking in his surroundings. He seemed like an old soul to Brynn, with wisdom and knowledge beyond his years. He never moved an inch from Brynn's side as they sat there. He was perfectly content watching the other dogs, and he would occasionally turn his head to her and look up at her with his kind brown eyes. Brynn stroked his black-and-white coat with a gentle, caring hand; his big, solid body pushed as close into her side as he could get.

When Brynn and Brewski started to head back towards the building, another volunteer named Jamie had Piper out in one of the big fenced-in play yards. Brynn and Brewski watched Piper from a distance as she ran so freely, not a care in the world. She was a beautiful, confident girl who Brewski couldn't seem to take his eyes off of. Her black coat shimmered when the sun hit it just right, and her ears bounced as she ran and played. Her smile was genuine and inviting. Brewski wished he could meet her but also was a little intimidated by her. He was shy and unsure of himself. He wasn't sure how to play with other dogs. And she was so…fearless.

As the pair approached the play yard, Piper was running along the fence, crying as she looked at Brewski, begging him to come play with her. Brewski pulled a little harder on the leash and led Brynn up to the fence where Piper was practically doing a tap dance with her feet, excitedly awaiting his arrival. Her paws pranced up and down in the grass on the other side of the fence, rising and falling to the sound of her desperate cries to play. Brewski sniffed her through the fence and wagged his tail. They both let out a playful cry and Piper put her front paws down low in front of her in a play bow position, her butt up high in the air, wiggling back and forth. Brewski seemed excited but unsure of what he should do. He cried lightly in excitement and looked back and forth between Piper and Brynn, as if asking permission to play with Piper.

Brynn saw the instant connection between the two dogs and it made her so happy for them both. She decided to put Brewski in the run next to Piper and let them have some fun. Piper ran up and down the fence line with a silly smile on her face, as Brewski watched and wagged his tail, ears perked up with curiosity. She would stop in front of him every now and then and jump forward at him with a playful bow and bark to try to get him going. Eventually, Brewski caught on and started chasing after her. They both had big smiles as they ran after each other.

They must have run up and down that fence together nonstop for 20 minutes. Brynn had never seen Brewski have so much fun or be able to relax this much. She wasn't sure she'd ever seen him smile so much. This was so good for him. Piper had brought out the fun side of him and it was so good to see. He had always been so bashful and serious. This was a whole new side of him. Both dogs were completely worn out by the time Brynn and Jamie decided it was time to take them back inside. But before they took them back in, the two girls sat on the ground on either side of the fence while Piper and Brewski sat next to them, catching their breath and getting pets and attention.

The dogs each drank a bunch of water from their dishes and chewed on a bully stick as a special treat that also helped to relieve any pent-up stress. This was what volunteering was all about. To be able to give these dogs the time to run and play and make friends and work on enrichment and confidence…it was everything. Seeing them run free and just be dogs was what made it all worth it. The time, the tears, the work…it was all worth it for moments like this. Seeing the transformation with these dogs slowly take place in front of her eyes made it all worth it. The joy it brought Brynn outweighed the heartache of seeing so many homeless dogs come in in rough shape week after week. She wanted to save every one of them and it killed her that she couldn't. But in this moment, she felt like she was making a difference in these two dogs' lives. She had a purpose, even if just for these two in front of her. She would save these two and she would help find them amazing homes like they deserved. It was a promise she had made to them earlier and she planned to do her very best to keep that promise.

Jamie asked Brynn if she had heard anything more about Sarge since he had come in the other day. Brynn said no, only that he was very old and had some kind of mass that would have to be removed, but they didn't know yet if it was cancerous.

"How could anyone do that to their dog?" Brynn asked. "He must be at least ten years old and he is absolutely terrified in this place. How could you dump your dog off at Animal Control before they even open, with a note that says you can't afford to pay for his medical bills anymore? How could anyone be so cruel? I heard he was tied to the tree out front and one of the staff members found him when they got to work. They couldn't even be bothered to wait until the place opened to make sure he got inside safely. People are just so awful sometimes."

Jamie replied, "I bet he didn't want to face anyone because he thought they would judge him. He knew what he was doing was wrong and he was ashamed. But there are so many things he could have tried before resorting to this. Do people realize what this place does to these animals' mental state? The confusion and fear and stress it causes them is unbearable. Especially a senior dog who has been a family pet for years, going from a comfortable home to a strange, loud, scary building like this? I mean, have they ever heard of a payment plan or Care Credit? Or asked their family or friends for help rather than dumping their dog? If it was my dog, I think I would take out a loan if needed. I just cannot fathom the thought process of some of these people. It's heartbreaking for these dogs."

Of course the girls knew that for some people, surrendering their dog to Animal Control might be the last resort and the best option available to them. In certain cases, it is really the *only* option to ensure that an animal is cared for properly. They tried to remind themselves of this, but when seeing an ill, senior dog abandoned and tied to a tree, it brought up feelings of judgment and disdain.

Piper listened as they continued to talk about Sarge and realized that they were talking about her new roommate. *Sarge had been tied up to a tree? And he really* is *sick? This was awful.* Her heart broke for Sarge. It was hard enough being here, but to be here and be sick must be brutal. She wanted to help him and make him feel better, but she wasn't sure how to do that.

After they took the two dogs back to their kennels, Brynn

asked Jamie, "So how was Piper for you when you got her out? Was she still coming out of her kennel full force?" Brynn chuckled since she knew how silly Piper was and how her dramatic exit from the kennel was just her demanding way of saying, *It's about time you came for me! Get me out of here now!* She could be a bit of a drama queen sometimes.

Jamie wasn't laughing, though, when she answered Brynn. "Not good at all. I'm actually getting a little worried about her behavior. It's getting worse, and if she accidentally bites someone while going after the leash, or head bunts someone too hard when she's jumping up, she's going to be the one to pay the price. You know that a bite would go on her record and she would legally have to be placed on a ten-day bite hold so no one would be able to even take her outside during that time. Then she would end up going cage crazy and only getting worse. We have to figure something out for her before that happens. She's way too awesome of a dog to have anything happen that might lead to life-or-death decisions being made. I feel like she will get adopted pretty quickly if we can start promoting her like crazy. She's so smart and is such a fun girl, I can't imagine it'll be too difficult finding her a home."

Brynn replied, "You're right. I will come up with a bio tonight and post it to our Facebook page for everyone to share. She needs out of this place as soon as possible."

Brynn went home that night and messaged Kaylie, another volunteer who was excellent at writing bios for dogs. Every bio she wrote seemed to get shared across the country and it helped tremendously with bringing in potential adopters for that specific dog in the bio. Adopters came from all over the state of Michigan and a few had even come from out of state and even *Canada* because of her bios! She had a magical touch with her writing that was sure to pull at the readers' heart-strings. Kaylie whipped something up in no time and posted it right to Animal Control's Facebook page for everyone to see and share.

Volunteers, staff, medical team – we are all worried about Piper. Piper is perfectly healthy but Piper is depressed. She has grown up a lot in the shelter. She has gotten bigger and wiser than the happy-go-lucky puppy that ended up in the stray ward. But with maturity comes the harsh, cold reality that life is not always kind, and it hasn't been kind to Piper. She came to us a skinny girl with half of one ear missing, so who knows what happened to her before she arrived. Now she's spending her youth stuck behind kennel bars.

When we walk through Piper's row, she doesn't wag her tail excitedly or even bark anymore. She stands quietly and looks at us out of the corner of her eye, as if she knows we're just going to walk by to pick another dog to go home and leave her behind, as we have so many times before. The Piper who used to prance and play with volunteers just leans against us, resting her head that is heavy with sadness. Sometimes she looks out the window, catching a glimpse of the freedom she fears she will never have.

Piper is too young to give up. And we're not giving up on this sweet girl, but we need your help. Piper needs love, more love than we can give her in just 10-20 minutes a day. But most of all, Piper needs someone to pick her. Pick Piper and show her that you want her to be a part of your family, because right now she doesn't believe anyone ever will.

PIPER. Approximately 50 pounds and estimated to be 1-2 years old. Please message our page to meet her.

Kaylie clicked on "post" and her bio was now out there. Brynn and Jamie shared it to their personal pages and from there it took off like crazy. Below the bio was a picture of Piper outdoors with a huge, goofy smile on her face, side by side with a picture of Piper behind her kennel door, with big, sad eyes staring through the bars and her face pushed up against the door, paws wrapped around the bars. Her sad eyes were all that post needed. Pictures of sad dogs always brought people in. And Kaylie was a genius when it came to knowing what brought people in, even if it sometimes meant embellishing her bios just a little bit...

The bio worked. People were messaging the Facebook page asking for more details about Piper. A few even set up appointments to meet with her the following week. Brynn got excited about the potential of seeing Piper go home with a great family to spoil her rotten. She was such a fun, special girl who deserved the best family. And she was still young, with so much life to share with the perfect family. Her fearless, goofy, loving personality was sure to steal the hearts of everyone she met. She was going to make some family very happy.

The first meet-and-greet scheduled with Piper was a young married couple, with no other animals and no kids. The perfect adopters on paper. They had seen her pictures and bio on Facebook and knew right away that they had to meet her. They were so excited to get their first dog. Piper initially did great in the meet. She came out with a volunteer to meet the young couple and walked right up to them to check them out. She was being her usual self, turning up the charm and laying it on thick with the couple. They sat right down on the ground with her and petted her and she seemed to really like them. They interacted with her for about 20 minutes with no issues whatsoever. They quickly fell in love with her and wanted to take her home.

As they talked more with the volunteer adoption counselor who was helping them out, they asked all the right questions and seemed to be a great fit for Piper. But somewhere amid conversation, the couple stood up from the ground and something happened that turned Piper off to the man. Her demeanor changed and her body language suddenly revealed she was fearful of the man. She offered a warning with a low growl at the man and began backing up. She was communicating to him that she was uncomfortable and to please give her some space.

The man was confused and didn't know what he did to scare her off. They tried to toss her treats from a distance to regain her trust, but Piper was done. She wasn't having it anymore. The volunteer apologized and said Piper might just be stressed with the number of people talking around her, or it's possible maybe the man's hat or boots triggered something in her that reminded her of someone from her past. It was just so hard to know what these dogs were thinking because no one knew what kind of past they had before they ended up here.

The couple understood but they were very disappointed as they really liked Piper and wanted to give her a home. The volunteer assured them that they had several other dogs for them to meet if they wanted to come back another day and try again. But they left without a dog and Piper was taken back to her kennel to sit again. The volunteer commented to Piper, "What happened, girlfriend? Do you not like men? I've never seen you growl at anyone like that."

Piper thought to herself, *I don't like* that *man because he reminds me of the last guy who dumped me on the side of the road after kicking my side in for having an accident in the house. I don't know what happened; he said something that just took me back to that day when the last guy was kicking me and I just kind of lost my cool. And his boots…his boots sent me right back to that moment. I'll never forget those boots.* Piper hung her head low as she sat back down in her kennel, looking defeated. She began to realize that she had just lost her chance at going home with a great family, and it was nobody's fault but her own. She lay down in her kennel with her front paws stretched out in front of her and her head resting between them, her big sad brown eyes looking up at the volunteer who was speaking to her.

"Lucky for you, you have more people coming to meet

you this week. You are little miss popularity this week with all these people wanting to meet you. You got this, Piper; you'll be out of this place in no time." The volunteer closed the latch to Piper's kennel and walked away, leaving Piper sitting there alone with her thoughts.

Just as soon as Piper heard the door shut to her ward, she heard footsteps coming into the ward again. She heard a stranger's voice and another voice she recognized as one of the staff members who sometimes cleaned the kennels. Her head tilted to the side as she listened.

"This is him. Poor old man hasn't eaten or slept since he got here a few days ago. He's just totally numb with fear and is probably so confused. Owner left him tied up to the tree out front like a bag of trash. Note said the dog is very sick and he couldn't afford to get him the help he needs."

Piper then heard the strange voice talking to her roommate Sarge in a soft, calming tone, telling him it was going to be all right, and she would take good care of him and get him feeling better.

A few minutes went by and she heard footsteps walking back toward the door to the ward, but this time she heard the sound of nails tapping against the floor too. Had Sarge left with them? She heard the door swing shut and it was quiet again. Piper stood up on her hind legs and stretched herself as tall as she could, pushed her eye up to the small gap she had discovered between the walls, and looked around in front of and below her. He was gone. Sarge had left.

A few hours later, one of the staff members came back into Piper's ward to do her daily kennel cleaning. She said in a loud voice to Piper, "It's your lucky day, Piper. Sarge is off to rescue so you get your full kennel back." She opened the partition that split the kennel into two and Piper's living space instantly nearly doubled in size. She could see the mess that Sarge left behind. His entire side was covered in brown filth, like someone had taken a paint brush and smeared poop all over the ground and walls. She couldn't believe he had lain in that for as long as he did.

The lady leashed Piper and handed her off to Brynn to take her outside while she cleaned the mess. Piper immediately jumped up and grabbed hold of the leash with her mouth. Brynn held her arm straight out to the side while Piper held onto the leash all the way outside, a technique referred to as "straight-arming" a dog. As soon as they were outside, Piper dropped the leash. It really didn't bother Brynn too much that Piper did that with the leash, but she knew that Jamie was right. If anything happens, it'll be Piper who pays the price. "We have to get you out of here, Piper."

They went on a walk since there weren't any other dogs

outside for Piper to play with. Brynn walked quickly at first to keep up with Piper, and then decided to increase the pace a bit more. She started to slowly jog with Piper by her side, and Piper seemed to really like it. They jogged side by side around the grassy area by the woods as Piper took in the fresh air and smells around her. Their footsteps started to sync with each other as they developed a rhythm that seemed to flow for them. Every few minutes Piper would turn her head to look up at Brynn, and she always had the same big, goofy smile on her face, tongue hanging out and one eye wandering ever so slightly. Her ears bounced up and down as she ran. The gentle breeze flowed across her black coat like a ripple in a pond. It felt both refreshing and liberating to run through the breeze in the open air, no walls blocking her way.

She thought back to being lost in the woods and couldn't decide which was worse…having the freedom of going anywhere while struggling to survive on her own, or being locked up in a kennel with her basic needs all taken care of. This was something she would have plenty of time to think about once she got back to her kennel. For now, she would enjoy her precious time outside with Brynn.

The two ended up jogging together for a good fifteen minutes. Eventually Brynn stopped since she didn't know if Piper had ever run in her previous life, and she didn't want her to overdo it. It was a nice little adventure for the two of them, though, and a great way for Piper to burn off some of her excess energy.

They sat down in the grass to cool off and Brynn talked to Piper about being on her best behavior for these meets if she wanted to get out of this place. She told Piper she knew there was a great family out there for her, but she had to be a good girl and lay on the charm in the meets like she did with everyone else. Piper just looked back at Brynn, smiling. Brynn wondered what she was thinking. Damn, this girl was so special. Brynn gave her a little squeeze as she smiled back at Piper.

As they walked back towards the building, a male staff member named Devon stopped them and got right down on the ground with Piper. She climbed all over him, giving him kisses on the face and soaking up every bit of attention she could get. He laughed as she licked his face nonstop. These two had met each other before and had developed a special bond. Piper smothered him with kisses and rolled over on her back, begging for a belly rub in return. She clearly wasn't afraid of men. She seemed to love Devon, and Brynn had also seen her with her fellow volunteer Derrick enjoying herself many times.

Maybe she was just extra picky about who she liked and trusted? She sure was turning out to be a bit of a mystery.

Brynn returned Piper to her now full-sized kennel and put a peanut butter-and-kibble-filled Kong inside her kennel to keep her occupied for a while. Piper walked to the now clean "B" side of her kennel and sniffed around for a few minutes, thinking about Sarge and how he must be doing now. Whatever "going to rescue" meant, it sounded much more appealing than staying in this place. She hoped he was getting the attention he needed so that he wouldn't be so scared and sick any longer. She hoped he felt better and could sleep in a bed with someone wherever he was going. Sleeping in bed with her mom and dad used to always make her feel better when she was sick or sad.

Piper was happy to have her full kennel back again but, in a way, she was missing having a roommate. Knowing he was right next to her on the other side of the wall that split the kennel in two, was somewhat comforting to her. It gave her a sense of companionship. She would miss Sarge.

Piper in her kennel at Animal Control

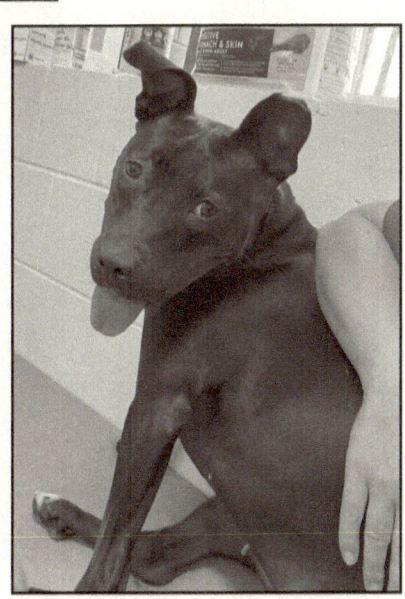

Piper posing pretty for the camera

Sharing a special moment with
Piper on a gloomy day

Piper displaying her
trademark smirk

Piper and I enjoying some time outside in the sunshine

A rare look of sadness and defeat from Piper

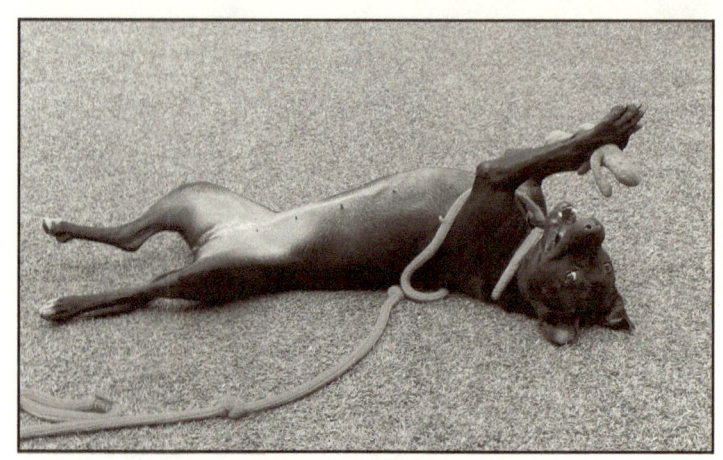

Piper and her green stuffed Gumby

Sweet, silly Piper

Brewski when he first came into Animal Control; my
first time meeting him

Getting to know Brewski

Spending time with Brewski in the rain

Brewski: such a
serious little man

Brewski nervous on his day trip to the park

Brewski enjoying himself outside

Brewski being carried back inside
by a volunteer

My boyfriend and I posing for
the camera

Spring of 2022

It was now early March and Piper had been at Animal Control for three months. She continued to win over the hearts of just about every volunteer she met, but she was struggling with shelter life. Piper became more and more difficult to get out of her kennel because she was getting so frustrated. It got to a point where only a handful of volunteers felt comfortable taking her out because she was somewhat unmanageable to leash and walk down the hallway that led her outdoors.

She also continued to be a mystery with her meet-and-greets with potential adopters. There was one meet where the family had another dog and it did not go well with the two dogs. Their dog didn't like Piper and Piper didn't like him.

Another family with two kids came to meet her and she ended up lunging forward at the man in the family.

The handler had to pull her back away from him on the leash. Piper made no attempt to bite the man, but her body language displayed that she was very uneasy around him and wanted him to back away. In her defense, the man was not making an attempt to go slow with Piper. He was all over her, putting his hands in her face and trying to play rough with her without giving her the time to investigate him. He did exactly what he was told *not* to do before meeting Piper, as so many people often do. Piper was wonderful with the two kids and the mom of the family; she just didn't care for the dad and she quickly let him know.

It was decided that Piper didn't like other dogs or men, even though those who knew Piper knew that wasn't always the case. No one could seem to figure her out. It was as if *she* was the one to decide who she was going to go home with, letting everyone know who she liked and who she didn't. She wanted out of this place so badly, yet she was almost sabotaging her own meets. She was an extra picky girl.

Everyone knew that having the label of needing to be an only dog in the household, along with her having issues with men, was only going to limit any potential for an adoption for Piper. One volunteer who loved Piper decided she would try giving her a break from the shelter to see how she did in a home. She took Piper home for the weekend and reported back that Piper was fabulous in her home! She followed her everywhere around the house, went into her crate with zero issues, had no accidents in the house, walked great on a leash, and even did great with her resident dog. In her words, Piper was "a dream" in a home setting. The only issue she had, again, was with Piper being uncomfortable around her husband. Certain men seemed to trigger something in Piper that no one could quite figure out, but others she had no problem with.

She brought Piper back the following Monday and the volunteers tried to brainstorm what they could do to help Piper have a successful adoption. It was being implied that she may need a home with a single woman. Or perhaps a lesbian couple. And she would need to be the only pet in the home. These were the only options they could come up with. It was so frustrating to Brynn because Piper loved so many male volunteers and staff members, *and* she loved playing with other dogs here at the shelter. Why should she be limited to single females or lesbians with no other animals? This was crazy! But unfortunately, they were running out of options and Piper was getting more and more stressed every day she sat in that kennel. They couldn't afford to send her home with the wrong family and have her get returned to the shelter…she would never mentally survive that. She was already declining and would never be able to handle going into a home and then coming back to this place. Time was running out and they had to find her a home before something happened.

Brewski had now been at Animal Control for a year and two months. The court case that he was involved in had recently been resolved and he was now up for adoption! Brewski still struggled with his confidence around new people and would not go into any rooms inside of the building other than the ward that his kennel was in. His kennel had become his safe place.

Every Friday, Brynn would get Brewski out first since he had been there the longest, then she would go right over to see Piper. Brynn would take Brewski out into the play yard where he had a huge yard to run around and play in, but he always chose to sit next to Brynn, unless another dog was out there for him to play with.

Brynn and Brewski had many conversations with each other about life, their fears, their dreams, and anything in between. The connection they had developed over the last fourteen months was priceless. He had taught Brynn so much that no human ever had. She learned how to be patient because of him. She learned how to listen better to subtle cues because of him. He taught her that trust was something she had to earn from him, and that if he trusted her, she would have to trust him as well. He taught her that she wasn't the only one with anxiety and irrational fears, and that sometimes it was okay to be sad or scared. He was like a best friend in dog form. She couldn't put it into words, but she felt this very strong bond with him. She had met him when he first was brought into Animal Control and now it was time for him to move on to a home with a family of his own. It was his time to shine.

The thought of Brewski getting adopted gave Brynn so much anxiety because she couldn't help but think he belonged with *her*, in *her* home. She didn't want to pass up the opportunity to make him a part of her family, but the timing was just so poor with her three dogs at home, one who was a senior with declining health. Not to mention, she fell in love with a lot of dogs while volunteering, so she often had to remind herself that she can't take them all home. She had to set a limit. So she decided she would try to find him the best home, but if he continued to sit there for much longer, she would take him home.

Brewski is my shelter love. He arrived in the winter of 2021. Winter turned to summer and summer to winter, and now it's

spring again, and he still waits. He is such an all-around great boy. He can be timid at times but once he opens up and trusts you, he will be your most loyal, best friend. He loves to run through the snow and in the summertime, he has a favorite giant tennis ball that he loves to run around with in his mouth. He has a serious side where he can be caught deep in thought, and a playful side where he likes to show off his athleticism. Brewski is such a special boy with a story that will melt your heart. He promises to love you forever if you will let him.

Brewski is waiting so patiently for someone to choose him. He is going to need a very patient adopter to help him work through his fear of new people and places. He likely will require more than one meet at the shelter. Please go meet him!

Brynn clicked "post" and added a collage of pictures of her special boy, and just like that, he was out there as being available for adoption. Now she would wait to see what became of it.

The Beginning of the End

Running and dogs. Those were the two things that were like therapy for Brynn. She volunteered with the shelter dogs once a week and she ran as often as she could. Running was an outlet for Brynn to rid herself of stress and to collect her thoughts. She had been running for years. She wasn't fast or great at it, but she loved the way it made her feel.

Brynn's phone sat on the holder of the treadmill in front of her. She was at the gym and was thinking of ways she could try to help promote Piper and Brewski to get them adopted quickly. Those two were always on her mind. The weeks kept passing and so far, the two dogs hadn't had much interest from potential adopters. When they did have someone interested, Piper didn't like them, and Brewski was too shy to even approach them.

This was going to be much more challenging than she originally thought.

As Brynn increased the speed on the treadmill, she started to get into a groove with her steps and the music playing through her earbuds. The smoothness of the belt beneath her feet hummed as she found her pace and steadily maintained it for three miles. Her favorite song to run to came on and she turned it up to its maximum volume, pushing herself just a little harder.

The music picked up so she sped up to sustain the cadence. She could see that her phone was blowing up with messages, but she wasn't able to read while running, so she finished up her run before attempting to read the messages. Dripping in sweat and breathing heavily, she stepped off the treadmill and glanced at the messages. It was a group chat with some of her fellow volunteer friends from the shelter.

Oh crap! No no no…this is not good at all.

She read that someone had walked into the shelter wanting to meet Piper that day, and a friend of hers tried to get Piper out to meet this person and had gotten bit on the arm in the process. It wasn't intentional. Piper barged out of her kennel full force like she always did and then jumped upwards to grab the leash but accidentally grabbed her friend's arm. It had broken the skin and her arm already had a large bruise forming on it. Her friend said that Piper had been very amped up in her kennel, jumping and barking nonstop with drool foaming out the sides of her mouth. She was likely stressed and frustrated after waiting who knows how many hours to get outside.

This was exactly what Brynn feared was going to happen eventually. It was only a matter of time with her level of stress and frustration being in that kennel 24/7. It was decided that Piper was too stressed that day to meet any potential adopters, and a "do not walk" tag was placed on her kennel until it was determined by staff if this bite had been intentional or not. The deputy director of the shelter would have to watch the surveillance video back to see what happened and talk to the volunteer who was involved in the incident.

Brynn's friend felt so bad for getting bitten when she did. It sounds crazy to say that she felt bad for getting bitten, but when a bite happens, the dog usually suffers. Even if it's an accident, the dog is put on what's called a "bite hold." A bite hold means that the dog legally must wait ten days before anyone can take them out of their kennel again. It was a Michigan law that quite honestly didn't make much sense. The dog is put on a ten-day bite hold quarantine and no good ever comes from that. An already hyperactive, frustrated dog sitting in a kennel for ten days is a recipe for disaster. So the volunteer carries that guilt when reporting a bite. But if a volunteer does not report a bite, they risk that dog biting again and seriously injuring someone.

Now Piper would be stuck inside of her kennel for ten days, with a bite added to her record.

Well, that news just ruined Brynn's run…

The Eleventh Day

Piper completed her ten-day bite hold. It had been determined after watching the video and talking to the volunteer who had been bitten that the bite was unintentional as Piper was trying to grab the leash with her mouth. The deputy director of Animal Control allowed certain approved volunteers to take Piper out each day of her quarantine, so as not to lose her sanity being stuck in her kennel all day for ten days straight. She was supposed to only get a quick potty break outside, but it was sometimes stretched into a little extra time if no one was watching.

Some dogs handle shelter life better than others. Piper wasn't one of those dogs. She wanted out of that place. She wanted the life she used to have with her mom and dad in her home, with a comfortable bed to sleep on and yummy treats and tennis balls and rides and cuddling on a couch.

This place was so miserable that she wasn't sure she could hang on much longer. If it wasn't for her volunteer friends and the few dog friends she had made during her stay here, she didn't know if she'd be able to survive this place.

Each day that passed she felt like she was going a little bit crazier than the previous day. It felt too much like confinement in a cell, like she was being punished for something that she didn't do. She still didn't understand why her family gave her away to that man, and why he pushed her out of his car. The more she tried to make sense of it, the more confused and angrier she became. She didn't want to feel anger towards her parents, so she pushed those thoughts away. She wished every day that her mom and dad would come back for her and take her back home with them. She wondered if they still thought about her like she often thought about them.

Day eleven finally came and Brynn of course took Piper outside to run. The deputy director of the shelter came out by the fenced-in area to talk to Brynn. She had a very serious expression on her face. Brynn knew she wasn't going to like what she was about to hear.

"I'm telling you this because I know that Piper holds a very special place in your heart, Brynn. I see you out here with her every Friday, and I see your posts on social media about her. I've been talking with the shelter behavior specialist trying to come up with something we can do to try to help Piper find the right home, but my options are limited. She's now lunged and growled in her meets with interested adopters. She doesn't seem to like men or dogs when she's in a meet, but she does fine with men and dogs here in this setting. Her behavior coming out of her kennel isn't good. I know the bite was unintentional, but I have to keep the safety of my staff and volunteers in mind. I'm kind of at a loss on what more we can do for her, and I wanted to let you know in case we end up having no other options for her. Like I said, I haven't given up on her yet. We are thinking about setting up a mock meet-and-greet with the behavior specialist and someone else Piper isn't familiar with, to try to get a better feel for what's going on with her body language during these meets. I just wanted to be upfront with you on what the situation looks like as of now."

Brynn wanted to cry. She knew what this meant. Piper had one more chance. If they decided she was "unadoptable" or a safety concern to adopt out to a member of the public, that would be it for her. She would be humanely euthanized for behavioral reasons, which was referred to as behavioral euthanasia. She would be just another dog who couldn't handle living in a shelter and ended up never making it out of there: another statistic. Despite what most people think, it does happen, but it had never happened to a dog who Brynn had grown to love this much.

She felt a lump in her throat as she held back the tears. She appreciated the transparency but couldn't disagree more. Piper was so misunderstood. She deserved every possible chance there was to find the right adopter, because Brynn knew in her heart that she would be a wonderful girl in the right home. For the right person, Piper could be the difference between depression and happiness. She was so good at making people smile; she could really change someone's life for the better. Brynn just couldn't stand the thought of losing such an extraordinary girl who could offer someone so much joy and fulfillment.

Jamie came walking out with Brewski a few minutes later and put him in the run next to Piper. The two dogs ran their hearts out, running up and down either side of the fence over and over. Brewski was so happy to see Piper since he hadn't seen much of her lately while she was on her bite hold. They had so much fun to catch up on. Piper teased him on one side of the fence, urging Brewski to try to catch her. Brewski would fall for it every time and chase after her until he was exhausted. The two eventually slowed down and lay on the ground on either side of the fence, panting and catching their breath.

Brynn told Jamie with tear-filled eyes what had just transpired with the deputy director and told her she was very concerned for Piper. They had to come up with something fast…a plan to get her out of this place. This girl was not about to be put to sleep under her watch. She had seen it happen with other dogs in the past, but never a dog with the potential that Piper had. It was usually an aggressive dog or a very ill dog, not a dog like Piper who was simply misunderstood. She would never imagine that anyone could deem Piper a safety concern. She was perfect, in Brynn's eyes.

After drinking some water and relaxing in the grass for a bit, Brynn and Jamie took the two dogs for a walk together, something they referred to as a "buddy walk." They walked side by side at a close enough distance for the two dogs to interact with each other, yet keeping enough distance to separate them if anything were to happen. Brewski and Piper sniffed each other and pawed at each other; occasionally one of them would play bow to try to get the other one going. One would pick up the pace and the other would follow suit. They were the most adorable buddies on this walk. Brynn was so proud of both of them. Brewski had shown so much growth and confidence since he arrived at Animal Control, and Piper had learned restraint and self-control, and was continuing to work on her manners. They were opposites in every way, but together they were exactly what the other one needed. They were an unlikely duo that ended up being fantastic for each other.

The two dogs would continue these buddy walks and play dates whenever possible. They quickly became the best of friends, and each brought out the best qualities in the other. Although Piper and Brewski were so different from one another, combined they were the perfect pair. They both cherished the time they were able to spend with each other and with their volunteer friends. They would look forward to this time all day, every day. Some days they would get outside at 10:00 in the morning and some days they wouldn't get out until 5:00 in the afternoon. The days and nights spent inside of those four walls were so monotonous, but this time spent together outside gave the two something to look forward to every day. They would daydream about their outdoor adventures to occupy the time spent inside their kennels.

Their friendship was something special to witness unfold. Brewski with his big head and worried expression, and Piper with her half ear, wandering eye, and silly smile. Two imperfect dogs who found themselves homeless and relying on strangers to take care of them. Two dogs from very different beginnings. To some they might appear broken or damaged with an irreparable past, but to Brynn they were both perfect in their own way. She smiled as she walked behind them, holding onto one of the leashes. She watched from behind as their butts wiggled and their tails wagged with joy. Both dogs were smiling, walking nicely beside each other. Piper reached her head over to Brewski and swiped his cheek with a wet sloppy kiss, then continued to walk.

They were happy and, in this moment, everything was good.

Preparing for a Home

Many of the beer dogs did not seem to be "home ready." These dogs had come from the worst possible background and had since grown up in a shelter for more than a year. They each had their own issues, and volunteers and staff realized that getting them into the proper home was going to be a challenge.

Every one of them would need to be the only dog in the house. Even though some seemed to be dog-friendly, it wasn't worth the risk of a possible returned adoption. Given where they came from, it would be best for these dogs to be spoiled and given the extra time and attention in their new homes. They would likely need some training and major decompression in order to adjust to life in a home, then maybe down the road a new dog could be slowly introduced. Getting returned would be detrimental to their mental health after being at the shelter for so long, so every precaution possible would be taken to prevent that from happening. There was no other option but to make sure that each adoption was going to be a success before placing these dogs into homes.

Brewski's major obstacle was the fact that he wouldn't go into any rooms inside of the shelter. He would freeze up if you walked into any room, and he would refuse to enter the room with you. What would that mean for him once adopted and taken into a home? This boy was *not* going to be put into a position of living his life on a chain in the yard again. This was something that could be worked on while he continued his stay at Animal Control.

There was a room in the shelter that was referred to as the community room that was quite a large room for parties and various events. Brewski would reluctantly go into the community room but was very uneasy while in there. Brynn would take him in there as a starting place to practice being comfortable inside a room. They would sit in that room for a long time. She'd let him investigate the room. She'd toss him treats and hot dog pieces, but he didn't always eat them. He was clearly on edge being in there, but he did as she asked and handled it as well as he could.

The volunteers who worked with Brewski came up with a plan to try to start walking him around inside the building to explore different rooms while he was out of his kennel. He had to overcome these fears of new rooms and people, or how would they ever get him comfortable enough to do a meet-and-greet with a potential adopter?

For weeks, Brewski was walked around the building, exploring and being pushed just a little outside of his comfort zone. Brynn sometimes took him up to the front lobby where staff worked behind the desk and members of the public were constantly walking in. She sat with him on a bench and just watched from a safe distance as the people came in. If anyone seemed interested in petting him, she would ask that they stand at a distance and toss him treats instead. He was learning that not everything new had to be scary. He didn't necessarily like it, but he did as he was asked. Brewski's fears were not something that would go away in a matter of weeks or months. The damage had been done at a very young age and this was going to take a long time to work through. But he was slowly learning to trust new people and always willing to try new things.

One Friday in late April, Brynn took Brewski outside for a walk. They walked through the grass and started to approach the fenced-in play area. Brewski seemed distracted. His ears perked up and he reached his head up to try to see the dog who was on another volunteer's lap inside of the play area. The closer they got to the fence, the more intrigued he became. When they finally arrived at the fence, he began to cry excitedly like she'd never heard from him before. His tail started wagging like nobody's business. This was not typical Brewski behavior. Brynn yelled out to the other volunteer, "Who do you have out here with you?"

At the sound of Brynn's voice, a small, blonde-haired girl with chewed-up ears and scars on her face peeked her head up over the shoulder of the volunteer who was sitting on the bench with her back to Brynn and Brewski. Even with all the scars, she was the most precious girl with the kindest eyes and the most loving, gentle personality. "I have Blondie; I just love this girl so much," the girl replied.

It was Blondie!

Brynn realized that this may have been the first time Brewski had met up with Blondie since their stay here. Little did she know that Brewski adored Blondie. He used to console her when she needed it, almost like he was her protector. He was an anxious boy himself, but he always put on a brave face for Blondie. She was like a little sister to him, and he promised her repeatedly that he would never let their owners hurt her. He knew that he had failed to keep that promise. Blondie had repeatedly been hurt over and over again, not only physically, but the mental anguish was almost unbearable for her. Her fragile body and soul had taken so much abuse.

The two dogs had gone through hell together, but she had been through much worse than he had. He was always there for her when she needed a loving friend to comfort her. He had often thought about her during his stay at the shelter, not knowing if she had been taken to the same place as him. When he saw her, his heart was instantly filled with happiness and relief. He had worried that not all the dogs had escaped the prison that once was his home.

Once Blondie realized who was on the other side of the fence, she jumped down from the volunteer's lap and ran up to the fence to greet Brewski, tail wagging fiercely. The two old friends sniffed each other and gave kisses through the fence, and they both were crying out of excitement and disbelief. It was a beautiful moment for both volunteers to witness.

Brewski lay down in the grass and stretched his one paw through a hole in the chain-link fence, reaching for Blondie. Blondie touched her paw to his and then lay down with her back to the fence, pushing herself into the fence to get as close to him as she possibly could. She rolled onto her back and her body scootched back and forth as she tried to push closer and intermittently stretched her front paws through the fence to touch Brewski. They both appeared to be so happy.

The two dogs stayed there for quite some time, as if they were catching up on old times, shooting the shit. This was the highlight of Brewski's day. He had forgotten how much he missed this sweet friend who he considered to be a sister. He would forever treasure his friendship with Blondie. And it couldn't have happened at a better time, because Blondie had just nailed her meet-and-greet with a very nice lady who was going to come back that week to adopt her and take her home! She finally would have a loving home of her own, something she had never experienced. The trauma she had been through repeatedly matched the outward scars on her body, but she would soon learn what it was supposed to be like to just be a dog. And she was so very deserving.

Blondie's adoption was the first of many for the beer dogs. It was almost unbelievable how many perfect adopters came forward for these sweet souls who had been through so much. Everyone had worried for no reason. One by one, these dogs were going home with absolutely wonderful people! It was kind of miraculous in all honesty, that each one of these dogs found such great homes. Some might call it divine intervention.

The adoptions could not have turned out better than they did, which was not always the case at Animal Control. Every dog that walked out the door with a new adopter left a whole team of volunteers and staff behind who could only hope for the very best outcome for that dog. For the beer dogs, there was a certain level of confidence felt with each adoption. These were solid forever homes, and it was the best, most rewarding feeling.

But Brewski remained at Animal Control, and Brynn worried he might never find a forever home.

When I was a kid, I was extremely shy. I would hold my mom's hand and stay by her side no matter what. I didn't talk to strangers and I didn't feel safe unless my mom was in sight.

That is Brewski.

Brewski is an unusual case at Animal Control. He has made himself at home over the past year and has slowly learned to trust many of the shelter volunteers. Slowly being the key word. Brewski has a not-so-great past where he was treated poorly by the people he thought he could trust, so he requires time and patience to learn to trust again. Once you've earned his trust, he is your best friend and doesn't like to leave your side. He has this way of making you feel so special, like you're the only person in the world who matters to him. He feels safest next to you.

You see, Brewski is actually one of the best behaved, all-around good dogs that this shelter has ever seen. He's just a fabulous boy that we all know would do great in a home setting. The problem is that he is so slow to trust, that it's going to take a very patient adopter who is willing to give him the extra time he needs. This will likely mean more than one meet with him, to give him the chance to get comfortable with you. It's not going to be an instant connection where he jumps onto your lap and licks your face and goes home with you that same day.

He needs time. He needs patience. He needs decompression. He is bashful and hesitant to open up and break down those walls that he's learned to put up from the people of his past. He will go at his own pace and let you know when he's ready to trust. But when he's ready, you will never regret giving him that extra time. He will be the most loyal companion you could ever imagine.

Do you have the time and patience to get to know Brewski? Can you be the person who gives him the time he needs to feel comfortable enough to open up and show you his true colors? Could you be his best friend who shows him what it's supposed to feel like to be loved?

Come meet Brewski and get to know your future best friend. You won't regret it!

(Bio written by Brynn)

Brynn had been sitting outside with Brewski one Friday afternoon, soaking up the sunshine. She wondered every week if this would be the week that it was Brewski's turn for a home, and she often asked herself how much more time she should give it before bringing him home herself. She couldn't stand to see him sit in that kennel for much longer, but she also wanted to see him be an only dog who could be spoiled rotten like he deserved. God knows he had done his time in this place. Brewski had no clue the type of loving home that was waiting out there for him, because he had never experienced a loving home. Animal Control was sadly the best he'd ever had. The thought never even crossed his mind that the best was yet to come for him.

Brewski had had a couple of people interested in him once he became adoptable, but because he was so timid and shy, he didn't spark any connections. He would typically not approach new people, so the first meet was mostly just to see him and become familiar with him. One couple came back for a second meet, but after taking time to think about it, they decided against Brewski. It was just going to take the right person who had the patience and desire to help Brewski work through his fears.

While Brynn sat outside with Brewski that Friday, another volunteer named Ally came walking out, saying, "Brynn, you're not going to believe this! A nice family just walked in wanting to meet a few dogs, and one of the dogs on their list was Brewski. I'm going to show him now and I'll be sure to point out all of his best qualities. Keep your fingers crossed that this is the one for him, Brynn."

Brynn looked over at Brewski, who was sitting next to her on the bench. "Did you hear that, Brewski? You have someone coming to meet you! You got this, buddy. Be brave like I know you are. I'll be right here next to you the whole time."

A few minutes later, Ally brought the family outside to meet Brewski. She had warned them inside that he was a fearful boy and would probably take some time to trust new people. She let them know that they would likely need to come back more than once to get to know him, because he was very shy.

The family consisted of a husband and wife and an older teenage boy and girl. They had read about Brewski on social media and had previous experience with a fearful dog like him, so this didn't deter them from meeting him. Ally brought the family into the outside fenced-in area with Brynn and Brewski. They stood at a distance like she had recommended, and tossed Brewski treats. Brewski sat right next to Brynn while they talked and showed no interest in their treats. They continued to toss treats as they asked questions and learned more about Brewski's past.

Brewski was being bashful as expected, but he seemed to take interest in the teenage boy. He started to sniff the treats the boy tossed to him and very cautiously ate them while keeping his eyes on the rest of the family. He would grab the treat then run back to Brynn's side, just like he did with Brynn the first day she met him in his kennel. The boy talked to Brewski in a soft, gentle tone as his parents talked with Ally and Brynn. He got down low to Brewski's level as he talked to him. Eventually Brewski came further forward to grab the treats the boy tossed him, as the boy started to decrease the distance between himself and the treats. He would come a little bit closer to sniff the boy when he grabbed his treat, then run back to Brynn's side.

After some time of repeating this pattern, he was very carefully eating the treats out of the boy's hand and allowing the boy to lightly pet his head. Brewski never approached the other members of the family, but he often went back to the boy for treats and pets. There was something about this boy that drew Brewski to him. The parents were thrilled to see the connection form so quickly between the two, and it ended up sealing the deal for them. They decided they wanted to adopt Brewski! They were prepared to adopt that day and felt confident enough to take him home with them if that was okay with the shelter.

Brynn and Ally looked at each other with tears in their eyes and simultaneously said, "yes, of course!" They made the exception for this family after seeing the bond forming so quickly between the young boy and Brewski. They were confident that this was Brewski's family that he had been waiting so long for. They had tears of gratitude but also sadness because they had grown to love Brewski during his extended stay at Animal Control. It was the definition of bittersweet.

Brynn was ecstatic for her boy, she really was. She couldn't have picked a better family for Brewski if she wanted to. These guys were going to be perfect for him. They were committed to giving Brewski the time and space he needed to gain their trust, and they were willing to put in the work if he needed any extra training. Brynn and Ally stressed the importance of allowing Brewski to decompress and being patient with him as he learned how to be a dog in a loving home.

Brewski would be sent home with a giant tote bag full of toys, goodies, food, a bed, anything you could imagine. The volunteers had sponsored each of the beer dogs so that the adoption fee was waived, and Brynn had of course sponsored Brewski. The family was so grateful to learn that the adoption fee was sponsored and to be sent home with so many goodies for Brewski. The only thing asked in return from them was lots of updates on Brewski.

As the family finished the paperwork, Brynn knelt down next to Brewski with tears in her eyes. She knew they weren't supposed to hug shelter dogs because, well, they were shelter dogs with an unknown past and they didn't want to trigger any type of reaction from previous trauma. But this was her boy, the most special friend in dog form she had ever made since she had started volunteering. She didn't care in this moment about the rules. She wrapped her arms around Brewski and gave him the biggest hug. She held him close for several minutes as she stroked the back of his neck and he kissed her cheeks.

"Be good, buddy. I'm sure going to miss you a lot. Thank you for being the best boy and for trusting me so much this past year. I expect to see a lot of updates from your new family. Be brave; I know you can do this. Have the best life, Brewski. I love you so much." Brynn kissed him on the cheek and with tears running down onto Brewski's head and a smile on her face, she stood up and watched as the family walked Brewski out the door.

The boy held the leash and Brewski walked next to him. They got about halfway to their vehicle when Brewski turned his head around to look back at Brynn. His kind, genuine eyes held her gaze for a minute. She knew he was scared.

Brynn waved and yelled out, "Bye, buddy! You got this!"

Brewski of course put the brakes on when they approached the vehicle. The young boy picked Brewski right up and helped him into the vehicle like it was no big deal at all. She watched as they drove off and she could see Brewski's big ole head through the window, his worried eyes looking back at her. The tears wouldn't stop flowing, but she knew this was a good thing. He would soon know what his life was supposed to be like.

She turned to Ally and gave her the biggest hug as they both cried tears of joy. "If that boy ever gets returned for some crazy reason, he's coming home with me." She laughed but they both agreed, he got an amazing family.

Brewski had been at Animal Control from January of 2021 to May of 2022. Nearly a year and a half and he was finally going home with a loving family. Within hours, the family had already sent pictures of Brewski sitting on the boy's lap on the ride home.

No more chains and no more kennels. He was finally free.

If These Walls Could Talk

Piper's future wasn't looking quite as promising as Brewski's. In fact, her days were starting to feel quite dark and dreary the longer she sat at Animal Control. She continued to sit in her kennel for several months with no hope of ever getting out of there. She started to accept the fact that this was her life now. There would be no more comfortable beds or couches with blankets and pillows, or toys to play with at all hours of the day and night. It was just these four walls that surrounded her for twenty-four hours a day with a brief allotted time outside each day.

She found herself wishing that Sarge hadn't been taken away to a rescue so that she had someone to talk to. Her good friend Brewski had just gone home with a nice family, so she didn't have him to run and play with outside anymore. She felt guilty for wishing Brewski hadn't been adopted so that she could have more time with him. He was her only close friend in this place. The four walls around her didn't talk and she longed for someone to talk to. She watched day after day as other dogs in her ward were adopted to new homes with families but always wondered why no one ever wanted to meet her anymore. Was there something wrong with her? Is that why no one wanted to meet her?

Piper was moved to a bigger kennel in a different ward in hopes that it might help with her behavior. A mock meet-and-greet was set up with the shelter behaviorist and another volunteer who was also a dog trainer. They observed as Piper was put into a mock meet with a person she was unfamiliar with, paying close attention to her body language.

Piper nailed the meet, which really did nothing to help them figure her out. The two suggested that they try training her with a muzzle to get her comfortable with the muzzle, to see if she would close the distance in an attempt to bite if she tried to lunge toward someone again. It was a safe way to gauge what her intent was when she lunged. She had lunged toward two men in two different meets with potential adopters, but with being pulled back on a leash, it was difficult to know if she would attempt to bite. So many people adored this sweet girl and couldn't imagine it was possible that she would ever purposefully bite someone.

Brynn never thought it was possible, and she had gotten to know Piper better than most of the volunteers. It became evident, though, that she was being labeled as having "unpredictable" behavior and was not being shown any longer. She was kind of like a "project" dog, so to speak. Until staff and volunteers could figure her quirks out and work on her behavioral issues, she wouldn't be available to adopt out to the public. So they tried to get Piper comfortable with a muzzle to evaluate her body language and intentions in a potential meet-and-greet situation with an adopter.

Piper did great with being introduced to the muzzle. Whoever was working with her would smear some peanut butter or stuff some deli meat in the base of the muzzle, Piper would stick her nose right inside of the muzzle, and eventually the muzzle would easily slip right on. She tolerated it so well and they continued to work with her on it as time allowed. She was nailing it and Brynn was so proud of her.

One of the volunteers noticed that there was a certain stuffed toy outside that Piper seemed to really love. It was a green Gumby stuffed toy, and she would lie outside playing with that stuffed Gumby for as long as you'd let her. She would toss it up in the air, lie on her back holding it between her paws in the air, and chase after it if you threw it for her. Brynn learned quickly that if she gave Piper the Gumby right away when taking her out, she would carry it outside like she was so proud of it, and it totally distracted her from her leash biting habit.

Piper was showing some improvements and was doing everything that was asked of her. This girl had so much potential with the right adopter and a little training under her belt. She was smart and eager to please. Brynn couldn't understand what the holdup was with showing Piper again so they could find her a home. For God's sake, hadn't she spent enough time in this place? Did they want her to sit here forever until she accidentally messed up again like she did with the last bite, so that they'd have a reason to euthanize her? She hated to even suggest this, but she wanted to know what the plan was for Piper, because it sure seemed to her like there wasn't one. She not only couldn't be shown to potential adopters, but the deputy director of Animal Control was no longer allowing anyone to foster her or take her out on day trips either.

Poor Piper continued to sit inside her kennel day after day with no hope of ever getting out. The situation made no sense to Brynn, and she tried to get answers, but no one seemed to have them. No one seemed to offer any help, besides the handful of volunteers who were doing everything they could for Piper. Over the several months of Piper's stay, Brynn put out plea after plea on the volunteer team page on

Facebook, asking for help for Piper. She had started to feel like she was fighting a losing battle.

A few of Brynn's pleas for help on the volunteer team page, where staff members and fellow volunteers can share ideas and ask questions of each other:

February 27, 2022 (when Piper was struggling with biting the leash and coming out of her kennel like a wild woman):

Is there anything I can do to try to help Piper out with being so frustrated? She is not an aggressive girl, she's just frustrated. I'm willing to try anything…a day out, maybe try a weekend foster? I want so badly to help her. I really really love this girl. Please tell me what I can do to make her a success.

June 18, 2022:

What more can we do as a team to help Piper succeed in her meets and become adoptable? I feel as though she should be one of our top priorities to work with right now, but I'm not sure that we are all on the same page as far as what we should be doing? Instead of being "unavailable" for months on end, wouldn't it be more beneficial for her to be able to go on day trips or possibly be fostered in a home? She loves everyone

she meets who is a volunteer, so why wouldn't these
options be available to her? I know I'm not the only one
thinking this. And there has been so much loss lately.
I really want her to be a success...

Her posts resulted in no help, which only made Brynn angrier at the situation. They were ignored by most of the leadership in the shelter and it infuriated Brynn. Piper sat there day after day in limbo, with no hope of ever getting out of there. Brynn didn't know what to do. She wasn't a dog trainer. She could only do so much, but her mission was to save Piper from this place. She could offer Piper her love and her time. She continued to help her as much as she could with her muzzle training and breaking her leash biting habit. She occasionally jogged with Piper to give her some exercise. They worked on enrichment activities to keep her mind occupied. Piper appreciated the variety of tasks and activities provided for her, and always showed her appreciation with her loving affection. If you spent enough time with Piper, you were guaranteed to be rewarded with kisses and cuddles.

Brynn had been a volunteer for five years and had never questioned the decisions made at Animal Control, but she truly believed Piper was misunderstood and they were failing her. She felt as if *she* was failing her. There was no reason why this sweet young dog should be punished by being confined to her cell for months on end while the people running the shelter were supposedly working on a plan, when everyone knew they clearly were not! This could not go on much longer, for the sake of Piper's sanity. It was driving Brynn crazy and even keeping her up at night. Two months had gone by since the deputy director had that discussion with her about preparing for the worst with Piper. If they were going to do it, why hadn't they done it?

Brynn watched week after week as Piper made progress in great stride, but she couldn't do anything about it. They kept telling Brynn she needed more time, yet the more time Piper sat in that kennel, the more she was adapting to life at Animal Control. She was accepting this as her life and becoming more comfortable with her daily routine there, which was concerning to Brynn. Piper was amazing but she would truly shine in a home. She deserved that chance to shine. Animal Control was meant to be a temporary living space until a home could be found. It wasn't intended to hold an animal for months on end.

Brynn kept writing pleas for help for Piper on their team page because she was concerned that Piper may be slipping through the cracks. There were more dogs sitting at Animal Control than Brynn could ever remember, so maybe she was getting forgotten or pushed aside. There was such a fine line between giving a dog extra time to show behavioral improvements and giving them too much time to the point where they deteriorate more, or in Piper's case, they accept the shelter environment as their new life.

Brynn was convinced that she was going to have to be the one to try to save Piper. She would fight for this girl with everything she had if it meant saving her. When she looked at Piper, she still saw the perfectly imperfect little girl who she met months ago as a stray with no name on her purple collar. She initially was not a dog who thrived in this setting, but she was starting to show everyone that they were wrong about her. She was conquering every new challenge that was given to her. And it seemed to be getting her nowhere.

As the summer months came around, Piper found a new activity that she really enjoyed to keep her occupied when she was outside in the heat...swimming. Each outdoor play area had a plastic kiddie pool in it for those hot summer days, and Piper managed to jump in every pool at some point during her stay. She would get in that pool and push her head through the water like a fish, doing laps around and around the small round pool. Sometimes she would take her stuffed Gumby in for a dip with her. She loved the water. It not only cooled her off, but it also made her feel like she had the freedom to move and lose herself in the moment. She wasn't trapped in a cell when she was in the pool. Her limbs felt limp like noodles, instead of stiff and achy as they often felt from hours of being sedentary in her kennel. She felt free. Nothing was holding her back. The cold water felt so good on her hot body. Having an all-black coat, she would get hot quickly.

Her routine became going for a swim in the pool, getting out and rolling around on the grass to let the blades of grass scratch her back, and then plopping herself next to her volunteer friends in the shade. They would pet her and talk to her, and she would listen, hoping for a little extra time out since she was behaving so well. Because she had been there for a long time, the volunteers would usually let her stay out extra time. And Piper treasured her time outside with them.

When they bent down to pick up her leash, she knew that was the end of her special time for the day. It was back to her kennel from there. Back to staring at the same four walls for another twenty-four hours. Back to holding her potty until her stomach hurt so bad, she couldn't hold it any longer. Back to immense boredom and pushing out the thoughts that she might be going crazy.

The thoughts of her mom and dad seemed like a distant memory she could barely recall, but she did think of them often. Their smells, their routine…she wondered what they were up to now with the new babies. Did they miss her? Did they know she was in this prison and not with the man they had given her to? She never stopped thinking about how great her former life was with her family she loved so much. She only wished she had appreciated it more when she was still in her happy home.

One Saturday afternoon the shelter had a big adoption event. Adoption fees were reduced, gift baskets were given out to adopters, and there was a bake sale happening to raise money for the shelter. It was a great day. Piper watched as more dogs in her ward walked out the door and never came back.

At the end of the day when the shelter closed and everyone was cleaning up, some of the staff and volunteers were hanging out in the hallway, laughing and having fun talking about the day.

Devon, the employee who loved Piper, was sitting on a chair with wheels in the hallway as Piper was being brought back inside to be returned to her kennel. "Hey, can I see Piper for a minute?" he asked the volunteer. She handed off the leash to him, and another employee was standing down at the opposite end of the long hallway, calling for Piper to come to her. Piper took off running down the hall, pulling Devon on the rolling chair down the hall like she was taking him for a ride.

Everyone laughed as Piper excitedly ran down the hall pulling Devon, having the time of her life. She was the life of the party at Animal Control. She was always up for an adventure or trying something new. The more she made people smile or laugh, the happier it made her. Nothing scared this girl, and everyone knew to take Piper out if they needed some cheering up.

She joined the small crowd of people in the hall as they reminisced about the day's event, looking up at everyone with her big smile, like she was a part of the conversation. By now Piper had been at Animal Control for seven months. She now thought of these people as her family.

A Broken Promise

The soft plush pillow under Piper's head was shared between her and her mom. Every morning when Piper's dad left for work, she knew that she had about 45 minutes to snuggle with her mom before her mom had to get up. She would move up from the foot of the bed to rest her head on the pillow and she would lie with her back pushed against her mom's body so that her mom was spooning her. It was their special cuddle time and it happened like clockwork every morning. As her mom held her close, Piper would dream of chasing squirrels and playing fetch with her dad in the back yard. Her paws would twitch, and she would cry in her sleep while she dreamed. Her mom would smile and hold Piper closer.

When the alarm sounded, that meant her mom was getting up to start her day. She worked from home so she was always there to take Piper out to go potty or check in on her throughout *the day. Piper loved her mom and dad so much. She loved her home. It was cozy and warm and loving and just…what every dog wanted for a home.*

The sound of the door swinging shut in Piper's ward woke her from her sleep. Piper was startled awake and instantly jumped up, half of her face smushed and her tired eyes squinting, only to realize she had been dreaming. Brynn was walking towards her kennel, but something was wrong. Why did she look like something was wrong? Had she been crying?

Brynn took Piper outside into a small fenced-in area and just sat with her there for a very long time. She sat in the grass talking to Piper about how special of a girl she was and asked her to please forgive her. Tears would come and go. Piper sat next to her and tried her best to make her smile, but it wasn't working this time. She wished she could make her feel better. Brynn just kept talking to her like she wasn't going to come spend time with her anymore. Could she be quitting, and she was saying her goodbyes? Piper sure hoped not. Brynn was one of her best volunteer friends in this place.

"I just want you to know that you are the most special girl I have ever met here, Piper. You make me laugh every single week I spend time with you. You are so silly but you are also the sweetest girl. You give the best kisses and snuggles and I just adore your cute little face. You try so hard to make everyone around you happy when we all know how difficult it is for you, living in this place. You have taught me so much about strength and resilience. I have never met a dog who has handled every obstacle thrown at them as well as you have. From the moment I laid eyes on you peeking behind the bars of your kennel door, I knew you were different. I knew you were going to be extra special, and I was right. You must know that you have done nothing wrong. You have conquered every hurdle and every challenge this place has given you and I am SO proud of you. You HAVE to know this, Piper."

By this point, Brynn was sobbing, her head in her hands. Piper sat next to Brynn with her head tilted as if she was listening closely. She was confused, but she just wanted to make Brynn happy again. She pawed at Brynn's arm and licked her face, whimpering out of concern and curiosity. Brynn managed to smile through her tears. Piper had no clue what she had even done, what was about to happen…

Earlier that day, Brynn had shown up late to the shelter. Her phone had officially died on her the night before, so she had to stop on her way to the shelter to buy a new phone. It was supposed to be a quick stop but ended up taking more than an hour. When she finally walked into the building, she went straight to the volunteer locker room like she always did. The usual sounds of dogs crying and barking followed her down the long hallways to get to the locker room. She noticed other volunteers were avoiding eye contact with her as she passed them.

She apologized to one of her friends for being late and explained that she had gotten stuck at the store buying her new phone. "I'll make sure to hustle so we can get all the dogs out today. I'm so annoyed that my phone went dead on me."

Brynn's friend pulled her aside and said, "Brynn, I need to talk to you. It's about Piper." She had a very concerning look on her face. Brynn followed her into a smaller private room and she listened as her friend told her about an incident with Piper that had taken place earlier that morning.

Piper had been outside playing, and when the volunteer who was with her had bent down to pick up the leash to take her back inside, Piper tried to bite the leash but got the girl's hand instead. She was trying to tell the volunteer that she didn't want to go back inside, grabbing at the leash to stop her. It was normal Piper behavior that had gotten her into trouble already once before.

The bite left just a small scratch on the volunteer's hand, but after watching the surveillance video, the deputy director made the decision to humanely euthanize Piper. She said it was too unpredictable if or when Piper might re-direct on someone in a home, and she couldn't take the risk of placing her into a home with a member of the public, knowing this might happen. Public safety was by far one of the most important aspects of Animal Control.

"Brynn, it's going to happen at the end of the day today. I'm so sorry."

Brynn listened in disbelief as her friend told her about what had happened. Her brain wandered off as the details of what had happened were explained to her.

No. This can't be happening. Of course she tried to bite the leash when they grabbed it to take her back in. She hated going back into that hell hole! She didn't mean to bite anyone. She is not aggressive or vicious; she's just frustrated. Obviously, she didn't intentionally bite anyone; she was just trying to grab the leash like she did every single time she went in or out. Why can't people understand that about her? Why did they make her sit here for months on end with no way out? She was stuck here with no option of ever getting out! Were they just waiting for her to mess up so they could put her to sleep and make room for another dog? Was she too much of a hassle for them to figure out? Hadn't she done everything they had asked of her, yet they still had it out for her? That's sure how it seemed. Or was it just her? Was she seeing only the good in Piper and not acknowledging her bad traits?

If only she had just gotten there at her usual time, she would have taken Piper out and none of this would have ever happened. Her most favorite beloved girl who had been sitting isolated in a cell for eight months was going to die because of a scratch on a hand? Brynn didn't think she'd ever be able to come back here after this. How could she ever get past this horrible decision that was going to result in an amazing young dog who was so full of life being killed? Unbelievable. Oh, Piper…

"Anyway, I just wanted to be the one to tell you before you heard people talking about it. I'm so sorry, Brynn. I know how much you love Piper. You should go spend as much time with her as you need. Don't even worry about getting the other dogs out; we'll take care of that. Just do what you need to do and know that we're here for you."

"It's time, Brynn. We're going to give Piper some time with her favorite people and then, if you want to stay with her, you can. But you don't have to," Devon told Brynn in a solemn voice. He had brought Piper out to the picnic table behind the building with a small group of volunteers and staff gathered around her to say their goodbyes. Piper had no idea why she was getting so much extra time and attention from everyone, but she loved it. She jumped up onto the picnic table and walked around from person to person, giving kisses and receiving pets and love in return. One of the nice volunteers even gave her some bites of her cheeseburger, and another one brought chicken nuggets just for her! Everyone seemed to be sad so she tried her best to cheer them up.

It was silent besides the sound of their sniffles. Piper wondered if they were saying goodbye because they had found a home for her. That would be great, but she was sure going to miss these guys she had grown to love. They were her family now. Her tail continued to wag as she soaked up so much affection from everyone.

Once it was time to proceed, Devon walked Piper into a small private room off the garage. Her tail wagged and she smiled as she walked next to Devon, having no clue what she was about to walk into. Her smiling face looked back at Brynn as Brynn followed them into the room.

Soft, calming music played in the small room and a blanket was put on the ground for Piper to lie on. Brynn immediately felt overwhelmed with sadness and felt like she might start to hyperventilate. The reality of what was about to happen hit her like a ton of bricks when they shut the door behind them.

Her tears fell rapidly onto Piper's black coat as she lay with her on the blanket and told her how much she loved her. She told her it would be okay, even though she knew she was lying. This was *not* okay. None of this was okay. She was so angry, and she wanted to put a stop to this, but there was nothing that could be done. So she lied again to Piper. "Everything is going to be okay, beautiful girl; you just lay down and rest your head on my lap. Dream about swimming and chasing squirrels and playing with Brewski. Everything is going to be okay." More lies. It was what Piper needed to hear but also what ripped Brynn's heart into pieces.

The first injection was given to Piper. It was supposed to relax her and cause her to fall asleep so that she would peacefully pass once the second injection was given to stop her heart from beating. But it didn't relax her. Not at first anyway. Piper started to stumble as she took small steps around the blanket, acting as if she was drunk and couldn't find her balance. She was disoriented and unsteady on her feet. *What was happening? What had they just done to her?*

Her eyes got really big and they stared back at Brynn with a mixture of confusion and terror. *What's going on, Brynn?* Her eyes were so big, so...lost. It was the look of betrayal and it felt like a dagger to Brynn's heart. Piper had trusted

Brynn and she had let her down and lied to her. She didn't follow through on her promise.

The two held their intense stare for what felt like several minutes. Those eyes would surely haunt Brynn forever.

As the confusion sank in and Piper slowly gave in to the effects of the drugs, she lay down on the blanket and Brynn held her close. Brynn gently stroked the back of Piper's neck, her cheeks, her ears. She continued to talk to her through tears, telling her to have sweet dreams and assuring her that everything would be okay. Piper's coat was now soaked with Brynn's tears. She was alive, but her once-vibrant body now felt lifeless to Brynn. That once playful, young, silly girl with so much love to offer was about to die in her lap. It was unbearable to take in.

As they struggled to find the vein for the second injection, Brynn was sobbing and had to get out of that room. The walls felt like they were starting to close in around her and she couldn't breathe. She wondered if this was the suffocating feeling that Piper must have felt every day she spent in her small kennel. She felt light-headed. She couldn't sit here with this perfect dog she had fallen in love with and watch her die for no good reason. She could not do it any longer. She had to get out of that room or she might pass out from the heartache she was feeling.

She gently lowered Piper's head from her lap to the floor, stood up, and walked towards the door. "I'm sorry; I just can't be in here for this part. I'm so sorry, Piper." As she left the room, she held onto the garage wall with her hand as she tried to catch her breath.

Brynn cried all the way home.

Several Weeks Later

Brynn tried to keep her mind occupied so she wouldn't see Piper's face every time she closed her eyes. She couldn't help but think about what went wrong. Why Piper? She had been volunteering for five years and every Friday evening she came home with scratches and bruises on her arms and body. It was part of the job. These dogs were cooped up in a kennel for twenty-four hours a day, except for the ten to twenty minutes they were taken outdoors. They were jumpy, bitey, highly excitable, and stressed. Of course they were going to leave some marks on their handler's body.

So why Piper? What had she done that was so bad that she was given a death sentence? Brynn didn't think she would ever truly know the answer to that question, but she believed that Piper had been failed on many levels. She was failed by her original owners. She was failed by the man her owners re-homed her with. Then she was failed by Animal Control. Brynn understood that they could only do so much and if a dog was considered unpredictable, Animal Control would not adopt that dog out to a member of the public. She understood that logic completely. They couldn't put a potential adopter at risk of being injured. She just didn't agree with the decision that Piper *was* unpredictable. She didn't think she ever would agree with that decision no matter how she dissected the events leading up to that day. So many factors played a part in her fate. The final "incident" was just the excuse needed to seal the deal, in Brynn's mind. She understood the crisis of an overcrowded shelter and a dog that had proven to be a challenge to find the right adopter for, but she didn't accept it.

The bottom line was, Piper *was* failed. She was a young, vibrant girl with a heart of gold. She loved to play and act silly. She loved to be loved. She loved to make people smile and laugh. She was so full of life and love until that was all taken from her. She sat in that cage for *eight* months. She was trapped. She was misunderstood. Brynn couldn't help but think that so much more could have been done for her, if only Animal Control had the resources and more volunteers to give their time to the dogs.

Brynn didn't blame the volunteer who had taken Piper

out that day. It wasn't her fault that Piper's life came down to this one small incident that left a scratch on her hand. She blamed herself for not pushing harder to get the help for Piper that she needed months ago. She was so angry with the facility who let her sit there day after day, just waiting for her to make a mistake. She knew her mind was obscured by what had just happened, but at that moment she despised that place with her whole heart for what they had allowed to happen to Piper.

Yet she continued to go back for the dogs. She promised herself and Piper that she would fight a little harder the next time a dog like Piper came around. She would push a little harder. She would NOT let this happen again. Part of Piper's legacy was going to be the *fight* she instilled in Brynn and the other volunteers. These dogs needed someone to fight for them; they had no voice of their own.

Brynn printed off her favorite pictures of Piper and framed them. She walked by those pictures every day and would always hold Piper close to her heart. She would later get a tattoo on her forearm of the words "run with me," followed by an outline of Piper's ears. It was for Piper, but it was also for every other dog who doesn't make it out of the shelter. Every time she looked at her forearm, she would be reminded of her reason for volunteering. These dogs would always be with her.

Brynn continued to run and every single time she did, her favorite song would come across her playlist, "Sanctuary" by Gareth Emery. She had always loved to run to this song, but it had taken on a new meaning after her experiences with Piper. It was a constant reminder, almost as if it had been written just for Piper. And here it was again, coming across her playlist as she ran on the treadmill.

Piper had experienced what it was like being in a family, and she had also experienced being alone and scared. She longed for her family but ended up finding her sanctuary at Animal Control. That would be her home for the remainder of her life and she made the most of that. She was confined to a small kennel as if she was a prisoner, but she never let that hold her back from being the fun-loving girl she was. She didn't let her unfortunate situation ruin her free spirit. And when there was no other option for her, she gave in to the medicine that she felt flowing through her body and let herself finally be free. In that moment she was truly…home.

Piper would always run with Brynn. Brynn would forever carry her in her heart, providing a new sanctuary for her to live on in.

Brynn turned up the volume and pushed herself a little harder.

January 2021

The black-and-white boy cowered in the back of his igloo, shaking with fear of what was happening. He heard sirens, and the number of voices around him began to increase the longer he lay there. More people were coming to the house. *Who were these people?* He knew his job was to protect the house, but at the moment he just wanted to hide in hopes that they wouldn't see him and they would eventually go away. But after some time went by, he heard the familiar voices say to another person who had just arrived, "This way!"

The faint illumination of the flashlight appeared again and gradually got brighter and closer to the opening of his little house, until it was shining full force in his eyes. He squinted and began to cry.

"It's okay, buddy. We're here to help you," said the new person who was wearing a uniform and held a pole in front of him.

The scared boy wondered what the pole was for. Was he going to hurt him with it? The man in uniform tried to coax him out of his igloo, but when he could tell that wasn't going to work, he looped something over his neck with his pole and started to pull him out of the igloo. He assured him that he was going to be okay and that they were only there to help him.

The black-and-white boy was crouched down with his tail completely tucked under his body and his ears pinned back to the sides of his head. The man in uniform held onto the pole as he walked him across the yard to a big van that was parked in the driveway. Inside of the van, the scared boy saw some familiar faces of other dogs who were living inside the house.

What was going on? Where were these people taking them? Was this what happened when it was time to learn how to fight, and it was time for him to learn? He continued to shake and cry as they loaded him up into a cage inside of the van and slammed the door shut.

The scared boy had no idea that he had just been rescued from his horrible owners through a drug bust that had turned into the discovery of a large, inner-city dog-fighting operation. He was headed to safety and this van ride was the first step on his road to finding the perfect home. He would never have to feel the weight of the unnecessarily heavy chain pulling on his neck again. He would never again have to see those two evil men who hurt him and so many of his friends. He was finally free from them…

The little black pup stretched her legs and yawned as she snuggled up next to her mom in the king-sized, extra-plush bed, wearing a pink sweater to keep her warm. She was only about 12 weeks old and had recently found herself as the center of her parents' world. They had come across her and her siblings in a parking lot of a grocery store, of all places. They knew it was a shady situation, likely a backyard breeder as they seemed to be everywhere in this town. But they couldn't resist her sweet face and her big brown eyes staring back at them.

They noticed that the tip of one of her ears had been cut off, but in their opinion, it only made her that much cuter. When they asked the man selling the puppies about it, he kind of fumbled on his words as he told them a story about how it was a big accidental scuffle between the puppies that had resulted in trauma to her ear.

They knew the story was made up and untrue, but they didn't care. They took the little female puppy home that day and spoiled her rotten. She was perfect to them. She slept in their bed, watched TV on the couch with them at night, played fetch with her dad outside just about every night, and was so loved.

For the next eleven months she would be spoiled and treated like the little princess she was. Her parents had thought they weren't able to conceive, so when they saw her in that grocery store parking lot that day, they both were ecstatic to bring the little girl home with them. She was the baby they never had but always had wanted. She was their whole world and was given enough love for a lifetime in those eleven months she spent with them.

As she stretched her legs and yawned, she looked up at her mom sleeping next to her in bed before shutting her eyes again. Before drifting back off into sleep, she thought to herself, *My mom is so beautiful; I just love her so much. This is the best life I could ever imagine. I'm so lucky to be able to feel so loved.*

And then she drifted off again, dreaming about chasing tennis balls with her dad. As she dreamed, her paws twitched and the right side of her mouth pulled her lips back, forming a small smirk.

Epilogue

Brewski's story is a success when looking at his life from where he started to where he is now. He grew up in the worst possible home that was full of neglect, abuse, and poor living conditions. He lived in constant fear, and rightfully so. Even though he had no choice but to live at Animal Control for as long as he did, because of the way the laws work when it comes to animal abuse cases, it ended up working to his benefit. He was given the time he needed to learn what it was like to be nurtured and loved. He was well fed, he had shelter from the outdoor elements, and he was shown affection every day he was at Animal Control. It was a slow transition because everything was so new to him, but he handled it so well. He gradually worked through his many fears until his bravery allowed him to just be a dog.

The day that Brewski was adopted was the day that he really began his life. He was given the best possible outcome and was matched with the perfect family. Animal Control was the bridge that led him from absolute hell to the best days of his life. It's an awful situation being stuck in a shelter for as long as he was, but Brewski made the most of his time spent there, always learning new things. He is doing great in his new home with his new family. They send updates regularly on him and he is just living the dream now. He has a special connection with his human brother that has helped him tremendously to overcome his fears of being in a new home. He most recently gained a four-legged sister, who has become his best buddy. Brewski is a survivor of animal abuse.

Blondie, Guinness, Brogan, Milwaukee, Donelly, and Shandy are also living their best lives. They were each adopted into wonderful homes with great families who keep everyone updated on how they are doing. Tula was adopted by a wonderful shelter volunteer and unfortunately passed away due to unforeseen health issues, but was able to know what it felt like to be loved in her final days. Blondie is so loved by her new mom and gets all the belly rubs she wants. The one who really stood out was Donelly, AKA "the Don." He struggled at Animal Control but showed so much improvement during his time spent there. He is now doing fantastic in his new home and his mom and dad absolutely adore him and spoil him rotten! The others are also doing well in their homes and their families send updates as well.

Porter and Killian unfortunately did not make it out of Animal Control. Porter had been too damaged at the hands of the humans who abused him, and there wasn't any undoing that damage. Killian was not able to handle shelter life and steadily deteriorated during his stay at Animal Control. Both boys were shown love and affection during their stay but were not able to be adopted out due to safety concerns. They were humanely euthanized, and likely received more love during their stay at Animal Control than they ever had in their short lives. It's heartbreaking but it is the reality of animal cruelty.

Brewski in a Lion's jersey in his
new home

Brewski in his Christmas
sweater for his first Christmas
with his forever family

Brewski in a sombrero in his
new home

Brewski's new four-legged sibling has helped him to build confidence in his home

A treasured inscription on my forearm that holds so much meaning in my heart

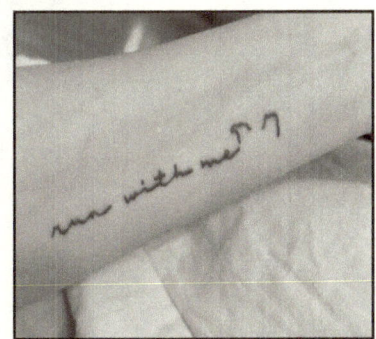

Random Thoughts
of a Volunteer

As I sit here on the couch next to my own two dogs (we lost one last summer, RIP Brinkley), it's still very difficult to reflect on my experiences with Brewski and Piper. Writing this has been a struggle because of all the emotions it brings up. These were two very different dogs with two very different beginnings to their lives. One came from the worst possible scenario where he was neglected and chained to a fence outside, among other horrible conditions. The other came from a very loving home where she was spoiled and loved, and she didn't know anything different. Ending up in a shelter was likely a shock to both of these dogs, for very different reasons.

It's important to know that when you are working with shelter dogs, you do not always know their story or what kind of life they had prior to arriving at the shelter. The truth is, I'm not even sure how Piper's life started. She came into the shelter as a stray with no known history. I created a beginning for Piper for the sake of writing this book, but the story I used of her loving parents giving her up after getting pregnant happens all too often.

Sarge is another one whose story I created, but his terrible story is not unique to Sarge's character. People dump their dogs at Animal Control all the time. In fact, I've been at Animal Control when a dog was tied to the tree in the front yard before the building opened. I watched from afar in disbelief as the man tied his dog up to the tree and drove off. This happens often. Just recently two dogs were found left in one of the fenced-in play areas with blankets and food, likely dropped off in the middle of the night so as not to be seen. Brewski's past, unfortunately, *is* known and is accurate in this book. Dog fighting...another thing that happens all too often.

I tried to emphasize in this book that each shelter dog has a story, a beginning. We must consider all of the various upbringings these dogs may have had while handling them, as volunteers. It is our responsibility, or I'd prefer to say *opportunity*, to help these dogs transition into their temporary stay at the shelter and again into a new forever home. We care for them while they're with us by feeding them and providing shelter, but more importantly, we show them affection, love, and various training tools to take with them when they move on to a new home. We are all they have, and they look to us for every little detail of their day while they are there with us.

I can't stress enough how important it is to these dogs to have people volunteer their time with them, whether through walking the dogs, fostering, transporting, counseling potential adopters, doing the dishes at the shelter, filling Kongs for the dogs…the list goes on and on. These dogs *need* us. *We* are their voice. We become a part of their story that might just help us as much as it helps them.

Piper will always weigh heavy on my mind and in my heart. If I'm being honest, my heart is a mess over Piper and it has been for quite some time. I have so many regrets that continue to haunt me with Piper. I wish I had done more to get her out of there. I wish I had attempted to bring her into my own home to see if she would fit in with our pack. The timing wasn't good, but what if it had worked? I'll never know now. I only know that she was a fabulous girl with so much potential to make someone very happy.

Although Piper's story has a sad ending, I wanted to include the painful truth that many dogs do not make it out of the shelter due to behavioral issues. Some dogs just cannot handle living life in a cage 24/7, understandably so. Animal Control can only do so much. They don't guarantee a happy ending for every dog who is brought through their doors. They can't. Their mission is to help keep the public safe, and the decisions made on whether a dog is safe enough to adopt out to the public can be very subjective. Although I didn't agree with this particular decision, I would hate to be the one who has to make that call, and I realize that things are not always black and white.

As stated many times in this book, not every dog can handle shelter life. Some will thrive and some will deteriorate. Unfortunately, there are only so many workers and volunteers available to give each dog the time and dedication they need to get through their stay. There is so much that can be learned from Piper's story that I can only hope will be implemented in future decisions on a dog's fate. I will always remember Piper as being an extraordinary girl with the gift of making those around her smile. She left a legacy that I will carry with me every day.

Brewski will always hold the title of being the "most special boy" at Animal Control for me. I have had many canine boyfriends in my years of volunteering, but he will have my heart forever. His journey and his resilience bring tears to my eyes and a smile to my face every time I think about him. His kind, worried eyes are ingrained into my soul and I hope they never leave. From a fearful dog chained outside to living in a shelter for nearly a year and a half, to thriving in a home with a wonderful family...he is the reason I volunteer. I see the updates his family sends, and I can't help but smile. My personal favorite update was his holiday photo. He was gifted a Christmas sweater and sported it on a card sent out for the holidays. What a handsome gentleman he was in his sweater! He truly ended up with everything he always deserved. I am so proud of that boy and I will always think of him as being so brave and forgiving.

These are just two examples of dogs I've come across while volunteering for an animal shelter. I used Piper and Brewski in this book mainly because I grew to love both of these dogs so very much. My phone is filled with thousands of pictures of shelter dogs, but these are the only two dogs who each have their own *album* in my photos. Only one dog (Piper) out of the thousands I've met holds a permanent inscription on my forearm as a reminder of all those who have not made it out of Animal Control. Piper and Brewski were both dogs that I could see myself adopting, had the timing been better. But I also used these two because they were so different. I wanted to show that dogs of all kinds end up homeless and find themselves in a shelter environment.

Being an inner-city shelter, the place I volunteer for sees a LOT of pit bulls. But I have also seen German shepherds, labs, mastiffs, dobermans, beagles, hounds, even corgis and golden retrievers! The list goes on. Any breed of dog is at risk of ending up in a shelter for circumstantial reasons that aren't always the fault of their owner. Many times it is irresponsibility of the owner, but it could also be simply that the owner passed away and did not have any family to take their dog.

The backgrounds of shelter dogs are also very different. Some will come from a loving home while others come from abusive or neglectful homes. Some come in practically starved to death while others come in fat and happy. Some are terrified and others are not. Some are puppies while others are seniors. They each have a story that we do not always know. They each have their own personality. These are living creatures that I wish with all of my heart could all go to amazing homes.

I wish more people would walk through their local animal shelter before paying thousands of dollars at a breeder for a pure bred puppy. I will admit that I was that person at one time. I was oblivious to what goes on in the world of animal shelters and rescues. My husband wanted a golden retriever for the longest time, so we went to a breeder and got one. I didn't understand why people would say "adopt, don't shop." Why were we being made to feel bad that we wanted a golden retriever puppy? I didn't get it. I didn't know that if I just put in a little effort and research, I likely could have found a golden retriever rescue. I didn't know that I might fall in love with all kinds of different breeds by simply exposing myself to them. And I certainly didn't know that my favorite breed and two of my own babies would end up being pit bulls!

It all comes down to educating yourself and seeing with your own eyes what these poor animals are going through. Expose yourself to the reality of the national shelter crisis we are in, because it *is* a crisis. Shelters everywhere are overflowing with nowhere to put incoming dogs. Dogs are being put down to make space for more dogs. Their faces need to be seen; their stories heard. My heart breaks for so many of these dogs who are scared and alone, suffering through their own mental torment and fears because they were failed by their owners. They have done nothing wrong, yet they suffer.

I challenge each one of you to walk down the halls at your local animal shelter before going to a breeder. Look into the eyes of each dog you pass through the metal bars of their cages and tell me they aren't as good as a pure bred dog. These dogs deserve so much better. They deserve to be treated with kindness, respect, and humanity. They will appreciate you more than you could ever possibly know just by giving them your time and compassion. Volunteering truly does open your eyes to the cruelty of our world. The horrible people who treat living animals like property; innocent animals who can't speak up for themselves. It's sickening and it will tear at your heart.

My hope for this book is that it opens the eyes of people who are oblivious to what goes on in animal shelters, like I once was myself. I hope that it brings awareness to animal cruelty and the need for better laws against it. I hope that it brings awareness to the thousands upon thousands of innocent dogs who are in desperate need of homes, and the need for stricter regulations for breeders. I hope that by reading this book, it inspires even just one person to start volunteering their time at their local animal shelter, or one person to adopt a shelter dog.

My biggest hope for this book is to always carry on the memories of both Piper and Brewski. I tried to capture their personalities as best I could so they could touch your heart as they touched mine. To this day, it never fails that every time I go out for a run, that same song comes across my playlist to remind me of my two most special shelter dogs. It's a constant reminder to never quit no matter how difficult volunteering can be, because the good outweighs the bad by a landslide. I know for a fact that both Piper and Brewski will always and forever run with me...

"The world would be a nicer place if everyone had the ability to love as unconditionally as a dog."
—M.K. Clinton

How *You* Can Make a Difference

VOLUNTEER

Call or stop by your local animal shelter. Ask for details on how you can become a volunteer. Many places will require you take an orientation course and possibly shadow a current volunteer to learn the ropes. Dogs aren't your thing? Check out the cats! They could use some snuggling and attention too. If you don't think you want to work directly with the animals, but still want to help, there are so many other things you can help with! To name a few: laundry, dishes, filling Kongs, filling water dishes, assisting with baths, assisting with social media, planning events, plus so much more.

ADOPT

Thinking about adding a new furry member to your family? Check out your local animal shelter, humane society, or rescue to see if they might have a good match for your family. Adopted pets are so appreciative...you will not regret it!

DONATE

Donations are always so appreciated! Most shelters can always use dog or cat food, blankets, beds, toys, and other supplies. Many places will have a "wish list" of items they are in need of, to make it easier. Money is always appreciated too.

TRANSPORT

Transporters to drive the dogs or cats to their next destination are always a need. In a large shelter like the Animal Control I volunteer at, we are constantly finding rescues to pull dogs who are in need of medical attention or who need more attention than we can give them. Sometimes a rescue will send someone to pick up the animal but other times we are responsible for getting them to where they need to go. Without a driver, they won't get there.

SHARE

Follow your local shelter or rescue on social media, and SHARE, share, share their posts! Social media is such a powerful tool in helping to get these animals adopted and into homes. One single post about a shelter pet could get thousands of shares and likes. So many people come into Animal Control requesting to meet a particular dog that they read a post about on social media. It really does work.

FOSTER

Sign up to be a foster. Our fosters are our most valued volunteers (well, we value *all* of our volunteers but fosters are simply amazing)! For every animal who is pulled by a foster, a kennel is opened up for another animal to take their place. For that animal who is being fostered, it could literally save their life. When we notice that a dog is struggling, we put out a desperate plea for a foster to take that dog out of the shelter to give them a break, let them decompress in a home, and see how they do in a home. A lot of times a struggling, stressed dog in a shelter is a totally different dog in a home setting. By seeing what they're like in a home, it gives us so much more information about them that we can use to try to promote them for adoption. Fosters are truly amazing people. I am in awe of the dedication and love they provide. They are 100% life savers for so many dogs.

And last but not least…
Read my book

By purchasing and reading this book, you are already supporting the shelter dogs! A portion of every book sold will be donated to the shelter dogs to help with whatever their current needs are. I truly appreciate your purchase and your time spent reading my book. *Run With Me* was an idea I came up with on a whim that has been so therapeutic and fulfilling for me to write. I hope Piper and Brewski have touched your hearts as much as they have mine.